EXPECTATIONS

Insights into the Power within You to Minimize the Effects of Life's Shortfalls

Colleen Pilling

Trafford
PUBLISHING

Order this book online at www.trafford.com/07-1121
or email orders@trafford.com

Most Trafford titles are also available at major online book retailers.
Brain Gym ® is a Registered Trademark of the Educational Kinesiology Foundation.
Cover design by Colleen Pilling, photographed by Martin Hansen
Edited by Tara Fleming

Note for Librarians: A cataloguing record for this book is available from Library
and Archives Canada at www.collectionscanada.ca/amicus/index-e.html

Printed in Victoria, BC, Canada.

ISBN: 978-1-4251-3076-3

*We at Trafford believe that it is the responsibility of us all, as both individuals
and corporations, to make choices that are environmentally and socially sound.
You, in turn, are supporting this responsible conduct each time you purchase a
Trafford book, or make use of our publishing services. To find out how you are
helping, please visit www.trafford.com/responsiblepublishing.html*

*Our mission is to efficiently provide the world's finest, most comprehensive
book publishing service, enabling every author to experience success.
To find out how to publish your book, your way, and have it available
worldwide, visit us online at www.trafford.com/10510*

Trafford
PUBLISHING™ www.trafford.com

North America & international
toll-free: 1 888 232 4444 (USA & Canada)
phone: 250 383 6864 ♦ fax: 250 383 6804 ♦ email: info@trafford.com

The United Kingdom & Europe
phone: +44 (0)1865 722 113 ♦ local rate: 0845 230 9601
facsimile: +44 (0)1865 722 868 ♦ email: info.uk@trafford.com

10 9 8 7 6 5 4 3 2

I dedicate this book to my parents who brought me into this beautiful world that I might learn the lessons of life. The dedication extends to my husband Wayne and my children Patsy, Pamela, Wendy and Steven who blessed me by teaching me about being a mother as well as their father who partnered with me on my parenting journey.

I want to include the spouses of my children who taught me the art of being a mother in-law and all my grandchildren and great grandchildren through which come the culmination of the precious rewards of family relationships.

ACKNOWLEDGMENTS

I wish to thank all my family and friends who gave me encouragement and contributed to the motivation to get my stories, knowledge and experience into print. I am grateful for the inspiration and guidance of my mentor, Dr. Carla Hannaford who helped to transform my trust in the Edu-K (Educational Kinesiology) process to a knowledge and belief.

A special thank you to my instructor and author, Kathryn Jensen, who helped me learn the art of writing and gave me the confidence I needed to launch this project. Love and thanks to Tara Fleming, for her expertise in doing the final editing adding a professional touch to the manuscript. Gratitude goes to Martin Hansen, my friend and colleague of many years, for doing the photography of the layout on the cover.

My love and appreciation go to my husband Wayne for his patience as I took the time required to write; for the discussions, critiquing, input and reassurance when I needed it.

CONTENTS

INTRODUCTION

I decided to write this book for several reasons, but the decision came mostly because of the urging of my family and friends. They have repeatedly pointed out that given the challenges experienced, I have handled life exceptionally well.

Entertaining the thought of sharing my experiences through writing a book began to intrigue me. Perhaps those who read it may find some of what I have learned helpful in solving their own life's challenges. Additionally, I have always found writing to be very therapeutic, using it as a way to express and process my feelings. It has been especially helpful when I have really needed someone to listen and understand me and there seemed to be no one available with the interest, patience or time for me.

Being in my sixties, I have been around the block a few times, so to speak. My overall observation has been that we form certain expectations of life similar to the expectations we begin to develop when we receive a gift. There it is, all wrapped with colored paper and tied with a ribbon. The anticipation and curiosity about what is inside begins to excite us. Unwrapped, we see that it is either something we have been long-ing for or some item that could be used and enjoyed. Gratitude begins to swell up inside toward the one who spent time thinking of us and then went to the trouble that giving a gift takes. Disappointment might be the feeling we experience if the gift turns out to be something we were not anticipating, or an item we already have, or the wrong color, size, etc. Often we ask ourselves, "How can I put this to use? Do I need to put it into my gift recycle box?"

When life gives us something different than we expected we have the choice of being upset, disap-pointed and angry, or putting our energy into solu-tions. I have learned that life doesn't always give us what we want but rather **_what we need_**. I have found that, although it is important for us to form expecta-tions, for out of them come our hopes and dreams, sometimes they become unrealistic and even our measure of success.

How we handle the difference between what we expect and what actually happens, determines the degree of joy and happiness we experience.

As a friend often says, "Happiness is a choice and I choose to be happy." Irving Berlin is quoted as saying, "Life is 10 percent what you make it and 90 percent how you take it."

It is my hope and prayer that reading _"Expectations"_ will encourage you and give you more insights into handling the unexpected in your life in a way that will better support you.

EXPECTATIONS
PROLOGUE

"Your son will never learn to read past a Grade three level." The statement from my son's teacher hit me like a punch in the stomach. From the time he was born his father and I saw great potential in him. His intelligence had astounded us at times. Sometimes from him came words of wisdom far beyond his years. As he looked through the books we had read to him he would recite the words he had heard again and again so that sometimes one could conclude he was actually reading. Hearing that he was learning disabled was unbelievable. But the teachers were the experts. What did we know?

We then began to search out find help for our son

in the school system. It actually took about three years before I finally admitted that I had to go to other sources to find answers. During that time I took several courses in childhood development, one of them from an associate of the Institutes for the Achievement of Human Potential. There are over 15,000 non-profit groups world-wide that introduce care-givers to the field of child brain development. The enlightenment I received through their courses led me to my training in Educational Kinesiology (Edu-K). It took me about four years to receive my certification with the Educational Kinesiology Foundation. During that time I traveled to many places in the United States and Canada in order to take training from leading experts in the field including, Dr. Paul Dennison, Ph.D, the developer of the Edu-K process. Many of the courses were taught by Carla Hannaford, Ph.D., a neurophysiologist and educator with more than twenty-eight years of teaching experience, including twenty years as a Professor of Biology. (Dr. Hannaford is the author of several books including, "*Smart Moves*", "*The Dominance Factor*" and "*Awakening the Child Heart*.")

Finally I became certified with the Foundation and could not only take on clients but teach the process. The whole time my son was the main focus behind my purpose in taking the training. As the processes and techniques were implemented, he gradually improved. The 75 percent grade point average he made in high school made it easy for him to enter college and while there he was on the dean's list.

Being certified made it possible for me to begin taking clients and I found great satisfaction in helping children and parents that were as frustrated as my son and I had been. Every two years I re-certified with the Educational Kinesiology Foundation. That is required so that all the counselors that use the process are trained in the latest research and techniques.

As I worked with children and parents, and progress was made, the parents would ask, "Will this process work for me?" Since stress is one reason why learning blocks can occur, the parents then began to relate to the stress in their own lives and how it affected their ability to handle situations that presented themselves. It was very rewarding during the 16 years I counseled, to be a part of the growth people could make through participating in their own progress. I have become very aware of the strength of the human spirit and each person's ability to overcome whatever it is that holds them back when they are determined to make changes.

While counseling and teaching, with my client's permission, I related personal experiences of others as well as my own to my students in order to teach particular points. All my education, my own growth experiences and the experiences of others have become the foundation of this book.

"Expectations" is a book where you will find many of your life situations mirrored. The first chapter deals with relationships between children and their parents. The years we spend growing up have a profound effect on the life we will live as an adult. The expectations our parents placed on us as children helped to form the expectations we place on ourselves as adults. Are you able to form only realistic expectations of yourself?

The second Chapter in the book helps to provide understanding into the development of relationships. How we relate to others is often determined by how we learned to interact in the first relationships we formed. Chapter three will hopefully bring the realization that it is necessary for each individual to take responsibility before they are able to resolve any issue resulting from their childhood issues. There is also information that helps identify those issues.

In the next chapter, the importance of creating balance in our lives is discussed. When we are out of balance, stress is the result. Stress is the biggest contributor to a lack of health and well-being in our human existence. Depression and anxiety are both products of stress.

Forming successful long-term relationships is the subject of chapter five. The work involved in participating in a successful marriage or partnership is addressed as well as the need to take care of your own "baggage" in order to be a contributor and enjoy the reward of success.

The next chapter, "Our Children Are Not Ours" deals with positive parenting. How can we more effectively raise our children using the best methods of our parents while discovering and implementing new more positive parenting patterns?

"Creating Closure" is a good chapter to read for insights into the transformation that must take place when we desire to move on to another phase in our lives. Moving forward depends on our ability to recognize that the past is over and make peace with it.

In chapter eight, we look at the roles that our education and career play in our lives. Flexibility is an essential element in any expectation and our life's work is really about realizing our full potential as a human being.

Finally, in the last chapter, you will find information regarding a variety of tools that are useful in letting go of all the "baggage" that prevents you being the person you want to be. Releasing the fears and negative beliefs that hold you back from really believing in yourself and that you are worthy and deserving of all that is good in life is **_so liberating_**. You can then form realistic expectations that will begin to attract what you want and deserve.

Every child is born into the wilderness of untrained, inexperienced parents.

CHAPTER ONE
EVERYONE WINS!

As Julie entered the counselor's room, she looked as though she was carrying a burden. Her shoulders drooped and the tension in her body was noticeable as she took the chair offered her. One would guess, from her appearance, she was in her early forties and the stylish business suit with her dark hair done in the latest style, gave the impression that she was well educated and had a successful career. Sitting down, she lifted her gaze to meet the eyes of the woman sitting across from her.

"What can I do to help?" the counselor asked, with a concerned tone.

"I have been doing everything I can think of to feel that life is worth living," Julie answered. "I have read books, seen therapists, tried to ignore it, but nothing helps. A friend recommended you, so here I am."

"Are you comfortable sharing what you think is behind what you are feeling?" inquired the counselor.

Julie paused for a moment before she answered, "Why not." There was another pause, and then she took a deep breath. "It's my mother; I can't be in the same room with her. She treats me like a child, and I am forty-two years old. Do you know, when I was young, she was voted *"Woman of the Year"* in the small town where we lived. But we never got along. She doesn't think I know anything; I have never received any recognition from her. My last therapist thought the only solution was to divorce her. Have you ever heard of divorcing your parent? That doesn't feel right either."

"Have you ever thought of forgiving her?" the counselor suggested.

"Forgive her?" Julie spat the words out with anger. "If you tell me I have to forgive her, I'm never coming back here again."

This scene is familiar to many people. Certainly the thoughts and feelings, if not the whole scene, will strike a familiar chord. Sometimes the difference between what we expect and what we get from our parents is the problem. Expectation and reality are often very far apart.

Ideally, every child should be born into a perfect

family. Each would have a loving, caring mother and father who have skills that would meet their every need financially, physically, emotionally, intellectually, socially and spiritually.

The reality is that every child is born into the wilderness of untrained, inexperienced parents. They are people who, themselves, have been affected and influenced by their own growing up experiences. Parenthood is one of the few professions where previous training or experience is not required to get the job. Even if one has had some sort of education in early childhood development along with experience as a caregiver, each child is very unique and requires something different. It would be impossible for each person to be prepared for everything that might come up in their own parenting career.

One also needs to account for the child's perception of his or her own experiences. Each child could be born to perfect parents, under perfect conditions and still have negative perceptions of his or her experiences. Any negative experience, perceived or real, becomes an issue. All of our experiences influence how we react to or perceive every situation in our lives there after. Children seldom understand the motivation behind their parent's decisions or the way they manage parenting. I once counseled a piano student of mine who arrived at her lesson very upset. It was obvious that we would not be able to get on with the lesson until her feelings were dealt with. After inquiring about her present mood, I learned it was over a conflict she'd had with her father.

"Do you know he loves you?" I asked.

"Oh, yes," came the answer.

"Do you think he made this decision because he wanted to make you miserable?" I questioned. "Oh no, he always wants me to be happy," she replied.

I let a little time go by, giving her an opportunity to process our conversation. Then I said, "Well, I think we need to realize that our parents' motives are always for our good, but sometimes their methods need a little help." The light came on, she settled down and we got on with the lesson.

Years later, as a grown woman with children of her own, this same student thanked me for helping her that day. Many times, that simple truth she'd learned through our conversation had fostered understanding between father and daughter. It had also helped her to understand that her own children often saw situations differently than she did.

I really believe that most parents do the best they can, with what they know. I can't imagine that any parent would get up in the morning and think, "What can I do to wreck my kid today?" then proceed to take action on a plan. There may be rare exceptions, but most parents make choices based on what they think is best for their child's well-being. These choices are often dictated by intentions and circumstances not understood by the child.

Admittedly, there are some children who come from homes where there has been some form of abuse. In these cases it is perfectly understandable that there will be issues. But we all know people who have overcome and even risen above their past and go on to live happy productive lives, while others seem to wallow in their past, allowing it to continue to pollute their future.

One of the most dramatic examples I know, was the case of a young girl who had been sexually abused by her mother's live-in boyfriend. When her mother was told of the situation her top priority became the protection of her daughter and the boyfriend was told that he was no longer welcome. In anger, the boyfriend retaliated by killing the mother. The girl and her sister were taken in by their aunt.

As the young child grew, she was constantly reminded by her aunt, "If you had kept what was going on to yourself, your mother would still be alive." So of course the child came to believe that she was responsible for her mother's death.

As one might imagine, a childhood like this would greatly affect a person's life. The initial experience would be traumatic enough, but the reinforcement and blame in the years following were very destructive. Even though she eventually married and had a family, many issues arose while trying to resolve the past. Determined to do so, she tried many methods and disciplines including attendance at workshops and self-help groups as well as seeking professional help. Through being aware of her example and of the eventual success achieved, the key to overcoming a negative past can be discovered by everyone.

There are those who are willing to take responsibility for who they are. The successful people are those who realize that happiness comes from letting go of expectations and accepting reality. They place more importance on what they *received* as children instead of what they thought was *lacking.* The winners focus on addressing whatever childhood issues they have that hold them captive to the past and then move forward.

When energy is put into solutions, we win. Putting energy into blame, self-pity, seeking revenge and anger diminishes our capacity to deal with life. Self empowerment can be achieved through focusing on solutions and resolution.

I was a child of the depression. My parents had two children, a young boy and a girl only five months old, when I was conceived. When my mother realized that another child was on the way, she panicked. Dad was out of a job and they could hardly make ends meet as it was. As a mother I'm sure I would have reacted the same way in that situation.

My mom and dad were good people who were kind, loving and dedicated to their family. I remember my mother sitting up all night sewing dresses for the girls. You certainly don't do that for people you hate. She taught the girls to sew, keep house, cook and mend with love and patience. In fact, I always thought we were rich. All my physical needs were met and an oft quoted phrase, used by my mother was, "Look how blessed we are!"

When my mother died, I was twelve years old. There was my older brother and sister and by then we had a younger sister too. My maternal grandmother stepped right in and helped all she could. Her philosophy was, "Everything goes down better with a little sugar."

As I grew up all the evidence that I was loved,

wanted and cared for surrounded me. I married and had four children of my own before the sky fell in on me, making it necessary for me to resolve my childhood issues.

At the age of forty-two I fell into a deep depression. It was difficult for me to function. I sought professional help. Drugs were prescribed and I tried to manage. Physical symptoms started manifesting themselves. I experienced early menopause with hot flashes and dizzy spells for which the doctor couldn't find the reason. I had psoriasis on both elbows to the extent that I was embarrassed to wear short sleeves and I could hardly function because of low energy. In fact, I would get up in the morning feeling like I was ready to fight tigers and an hour later it felt as though someone had drained all my energy out of my big toe and I simply dragged myself around the rest of the day. Discouragement set in to the point that I began to accept that what I was experiencing was as good as my life was going to get. Then I started finding answers.

My perception of my mother's panic when she discovered her pregnancy was that I was unwanted. That was not the reality, for mom had quickly resolved her feelings and looked forward to my birth. My first perception however, continued to influence my whole life. That is why, when mom and dad introduced their family saying, "This is our eldest son and our oldest daughter and this is our little mistake," I wasn't able to take it as the joke that it was intended to be. I internalized in a way that reinforced the perception I had now accepted as my reality.

Discovering the source of my depression unlocked

the mystery to my reactions in many situations and particularly my perfectionist traits. I had adopted the negative belief that my acceptance was based on my performance, coupled with the belief that I was unloveable. *"If your own mother didn't want you, you must be unacceptable in some way and certainly unworthy of love."* So in order to get love and acceptance I became overly concerned with my performance and had a hard time believing that anyone else could see it as acceptable. Regardless of the recognition I got, a little voice would go off in my head, "They don't mean it, they are just saying it." Or, "I wonder what they really want from me?"

Of course I had very little self-esteem and a hard time setting boundaries or standing up for myself. I was easily manipulated and always took on more than was reasonable for me to achieve. Long held emotional issues create stress in the mind/body system and eventually may lead to physical symptoms as well as emotional problems and I was certainly at that point when finally, at the age of forty-two, I crashed. I had worn out all my coping mechanisms. What made things worse was that I had handled some situations that were far more challenging than the one that actually caused the crash. I was really hard on myself for being unable to manage this time. Besides, when I considered all the reasons I had to be happy, they far out weighed my reasons to be depressed.

None of this was my parents fault. They had done their best with the means, skills and resources available to them. It was my responsibility to resolve the issues from my past. Fortunately, I succeeded. How

I was able to do that will be discussed in a later chapter.

Let's go back to Julie and her mother for a moment. What did Julie learn that helped her? She finally accepted that forgiving or letting go was the only way. She had understood in the beginning that forgiveness meant she must resume a relationship with her mother, going back to the old patterns where she then felt compelled to assume the child role. Gaining an understanding that she first needed to recognize her own worth and that she had many rights, gave her confidence. She began to recognize that one of those rights was to set boundaries, not only with her mother but in all her relationships. When strong enough, she could begin to develop and nurture a new relationship with her mom based on a good self-esteem. One where she loved, accepted and approved of herself at each stage of her growth process. She learned that her acceptance should be unconditional, just like love. Eventually, her own self-acceptance was all she really needed. The pattern of seeking acceptance from any outside source, including her mother, was eliminated. At this point, Julie would only accept or internalize love, acceptance and respect from those around her. If she felt other emotions being directed to her, she could screen them out.

Recognizing when others were acting out of their own issues helped her to allow people to take responsibility for those issues, and she only took personal responsibility for her contribution to a situation or circumstance. She learned to accept the suggestions, criticisms and judgements from others only as information. The information could be processed and a choice be made on whether to internalize it as something useful or disregard it.

Forgiveness really only means that we lose the desire for revenge. It also means letting go of the hope of a better past but still using it as a learning tool. Both require work on our part. Recognizing our worth and the power within us to resolve the past and move forward is the first step. Realizing that carrying a grudge or blaming others only gives the offender more power, helps in understanding that carrying bitterness inside only affects us and in no way punishes the other person.

Each person has the right to their own personal space, to set their boundaries and to be in charge of their own life. Each has the right to make choices for themselves to develop their own belief system based on their own experience and to set their own standards and values based on that belief system. We have the right to set our own expectations of ourselves rather than constantly attempting to live up to the expectations of others, including parental measurements.

In order to do this effectively we may have to question the beliefs, standards, patterns and methods of our parents. From there we can accept or reject anything that is out of integrity with our chosen values and standards. If we have been raised in an ideal environment where love, respect, justice, kindness and understanding were practiced, we may choose to accept most of our parents' standards, values and beliefs as our own.

Sometimes it is hard for us to claim our rights while

respecting the fact that everyone around us potentially has the same rights, including our parents. Finding our own place and being in charge of our own space, however, does not give us the right to control others. Attributes of understanding, tolerance, patience, compassion, forgiveness, and kindness need to be developed. When these attributes are firmly implanted internally, we attract others to us who have similar attributes.

Julie learned to set boundaries. In order to make the changes necessary, new patterns of behavior and ways of relating were learned. Julie and her mother now relate as two adults.

When we take responsibility, forgive others and ourselves, we can move forward in all our relationships including the relationship with our parents.

Everyone wins!

You can not change the way people choose to behave toward you, but you can change your reaction to it.

CHAPTER TWO
EVOLVING RELATIONSHIPS

Mom, Dad and me is the first relationship that is important to us and is essential for our survival. Mom and dad provide all our basic needs being food, shelter and nurturing. If that relationship is safe and healthy it is easy for us to move beyond that inner core and develop a bond with our siblings. Our grandparents become an important part of our inner circle and then we reach out to extended family members such as aunts, uncles and cousins. Each step can be taken with confidence if our relationship with mom and dad is secure. Then as we venture further, to the mid and outer circles of family relationships, bonding naturally occurs with others. We then feel safe to reach outside the family circle and include friends and finally, as we mature, we become attracted to a significant other with whom we develop a life-long relationship and begin our own family.

Our five basic emotional needs are to feel:

- **safe,**
- **wanted,**
- **needed,**
- **loved,**
- **and accepted.**

If any of those needs have been threatened or violated in the first stage relationship with our parents, it becomes difficult for us to feel secure in reaching out to even our siblings. These needs can be threatened even before we are born. Right from the moment of conception, the developing fetus is affected by the feelings of the mother, father or both. The sense of touch and the ability to sense emotion as well as the ability to feel sound, develops early. As the growing baby begins to develop its auditory sense, all sound is filtered through a fluid environment. Through all experiences with sound, touch and sensing emotion, the unborn infant begins forming perceptions of the world it will be born into.

A mother was having a lot of trouble with her baby of nine months. The young child, from birth, would fuss and cry, refusing to be comforted unless it was next to and preferably touching the mother night and day. When the child finally fell asleep it would only be for short periods and had to be held or cuddled by the mother even then.

Many approaches to finding a solution for the mother and child were tried. After several months, a discovery was made that the child was reacting to what it had experienced with the mother prior to the birth.

Soon after the child was conceived, the mother's father had been diagnosed with cancer. All during the pregnancy the mother was dealing with the emotional turmoil that accompanies the involvement in a loved one's fight with cancer, finally terminating in death. From the child's point of view, he was coming into a very unpleasant world where pain and grief were all one could look forward to. Once everyone began to understand what the child was feeling, the situation could be resolved.

The adoptive parents of a young girl became concerned when she began sneaking food to bed on a nightly basis. It seemed that she needed food to comfort her much as other children become attached to a stuffed animal or blanket. One could say, "Why would that be a problem? Just give her an apple to snuggle up with." But the parents would find a banana tucked between the mattress and box spring (after it had been there for several days), or a piece of chocolate cake tucked under a pillow. It developed into quite a problem. In finding a solution, research into the birth mother's background helped to uncover the reason for the abnormal behavior.

When the child's birth mother had become aware that she was pregnant, because she was un-married and didn't know how to handle her situation, several clumsy attempts to abort the baby had been made. One method had been starvation. Eventually she decided to carry the baby to full-term and then give it up for adoption - but the child was still reacting to the trauma she had experienced in the womb.

Because all infants are an extension of their mother and father, they are very sensitive to, and impacted by, the feelings and experiences of both parents, and especially those of the mother. That is why specialists in early childhood development encourage talking to an unborn child, playing music for it, rubbing the mother's tummy and many other methods of sending positive communication. This also helps the parents tune into the fact that the developing baby is actually affected by communication, both positive and negative.

Throughout the birthing process this little human being also forms perceptions of the outside world and because of its survival instincts, begins to create coping mechanisms. For most children, their pre-birth experience has been one of safety and comfort. But think of what is experienced by every infant for the first time as they go through the birthing process.

Even without complications during the birth, the child will experience separation from its mother and begin breathing on its own. Cold and hunger are felt for the first time. Air born sounds, light, and certain kinds of touch are all unfamiliar to them. It must be remembered that every person perceives his or her own experiences in their own unique way. One child may take in all of these experiences without creating issues while another may end up with negative perceptions in many areas that lead to issues. One may acquire issues with touch; another may perceive they have been abandoned through separation from the mother. Each issue has its own impact on the way a child develops its ability to inter-relate to those in his or her inner circle and most certainly these perceptions will influence the ability to reach out to the extended circle of relationships.

A struggle with taking the first breath of life often causes a fear that later interferes with confidence. Often a belief is acquired that a threat to physical safety is always present and there is a need develops to be on guard at all times. Trust would most certainly be an issue and in an effort to protect itself the child may be reluctant to try anything new. This would also include a reluctance to reach out for new relationships.

Separation from the mother sometimes creates abandonment issues. In observing the child's behavior, one might see a child clinging to a parent or the exact opposite, where the child holds everyone at arm's length, so to speak. Sometimes one or the other behavior is consistent and sometimes vacillating between the two extremes is evident. Abandonment issues carried into later life can cause a person to cling so hard to others that they end up smothering relationships or they sabotage them when they feel others are getting too close. Their subconscious tells them that ending the relationship themselves will prevent them from getting hurt when others might initiate a termination.

Basic physical needs being threatened often cause

deprivation issues. Behaviors evidenced when coping mechanisms were developed around cold and hunger might be an accumulation of material things or turning to food for comfort, among others.

Issues with the senses, such as sensitivity to light, sound or touch, can also occur. The light issues have been known to interfere with the development of sight and insight. It is also possible that the ability to listen and process language can be affected.

Touch issues can really interfere with healthy interactions within every circle of relationship development. Through appropriate touch, human beings are assured of love and acceptance. Touch is an important part of being nurtured. If a child is on one end of the spectrum, where they have to be held, cuddled and touched all the time then all the hugging and touching they get will never be enough. Often, later in life they may be easily influenced to experiment with sexual touching much before they are mature enough, intellectually and emotionally, to develop that part of themselves in healthy ways. On the other hand, frigidity can occur. Either extreme can interfere with the development of a healthy sexual relationship when the person is mature and ready.

Once we have formed a negative belief and developed a coping mechanism to protect ourselves, everything we experience is filtered through that belief and we choose our reaction to situations based on the belief. We often turn what is really said into something that will re-enforce or be in harmony with the belief we have accepted as our reality. In the last chapter I discussed my belief that I was unloved by my mother.

I confessed that I became a perfectionist to gain acceptance. The voices in my head, "They don't mean that, they are just saying it," or "They are just saying that to get something from me," came from my attempt to reinforce the beliefs I had already accepted about myself.

Our place in the family is important in the way we accept others. The oldest child has its own challenges. Very seldom have newlyweds had training or experience with being the full-time caregiver to a new baby. Education in early childhood development or even experience in child care seldom equips anyone for the full twenty-four hour care of a new baby. So that first child becomes an experiment for the parents and the pioneer for the siblings that come along after. The adjustment from having all the attention, to sharing it when a second child comes along, can be traumatic. Responsibility is placed on the oldest child as well.

The youngest child comes along when parents have learned what is really important to deal with and what is just a growing phase that only needs to be managed with patience. The children who occupy this place in the family usually feel that they are the last to get any privileges, which is usually true, because they are the last to take on responsibility, but they have yet to learn that privilege is earned through learning to take responsibility. Their desire is to get what all their siblings have without paying the price. Everyone else looks on them as the baby who gets away with everything.

The middle children often feel that they are never

noticed. Everyone listens to the older child and the youngest and they are lost somewhere in between.

I once worked with a young couple who had three girls. The oldest one had learned to talk early. The middle child started throwing tantrums when she was around three-years-old and the parents were searching for a solution. They had patiently tried everything that had been suggested from many different sources. Finally, the grandmother told them I might be of assistance.

During the first session the little girl was sitting in a big arm chair and mom, dad, and I were discussing the situation. Finally the little girl jumped out of the chair, ran to her mom and said, "No one ever listens to me." The answer came from her. Upon analyzing the situation, the mom and dad realized that the second child was struggling with speech and because the older daughter was so fluent and the younger was a baby that got every one's attention, she was feeling left out. Tantrums were a great attention getter. The solution was clear.

Coping with birthing issues and a place in the family often causes children to take on behavioral characteristics which some family system experts have identified as roles. Often these roles influence our ability to build healthy relationships while growing up and are carried into adult life. They then affect our ability to develop mature relationships. For instance, it may be evident that a person uses a substance, or process to overcome anxiety. We could recognize that a person has a tendency to make excuses for, or hide the mistakes of others. Behaviors that are clearly designed to draw excessive amounts of positive attention through high achievement, the need for popularity and the obsession with a need for having a lot of money, may be prevalent. One who constantly draws excessive amounts of negative attention to himself or herself through hostility, defiance and anger, could be using a troublemaker role just to get attention.

Then there is the survival role in which the person chooses to withdraw from society, is excessively quiet and makes little effort to interact with others. The final example is the person who uses both positive and negative attention to make changes to his or her environment. The behavior might be labeled as "showing off". All of these behaviors are evident to some degree in most of us, depending on the situation we are in. It is when the behaviors are excessive that role playing becomes evident.

All through our growing up years, our ability to develop friendships with members of our own sex and then with the opposite sex, our choices and experiences, have all been influenced by the perceptions and coping mechanisms we developed out of our earliest awareness. We expect that if we want to be friends, those we reach out to for relationships will want the same thing. We expect that if we give friendship, loyalty and support, that is what we will receive. This is when we begin to experience rejection, criticism, disappointment and even cruelty. Each person acts out of their own sense of self and issues they have acquired in their life to any given point. As a result, how others react to us, as we reach out, may be very positive, and match our expectations or the experience could be negative. If our sense of self is positive, we are able to recognize whether the other person's negative reaction really has nothing to do with us and we can give them responsibility for their own issues. If we have a negative sense of self, often we take responsibility for the other person's response and we choose to internalize it, supporting a negative belief about ourselves. Sometimes an old coping mechanism will be triggered causing some people to protect themselves by lashing out in certain ways or they may withdraw. On one hand, a war of words could ensue which might even escalate into a physical interface. On the other hand, some may feel unable to defend themselves and become shy and quiet, unable to stand up for themselves.

Now that I have lived more than a few years and can look back over my own experiences, I am able to recognize the importance of self-esteem and how that played a role in my success in developing healthy relationships throughout my life.

In my youth I had a very hard time making and keeping friends, while my sister had two special friends throughout her whole youth, teenage years and adulthood. Interesting how two people can grow up in the same family under the same circumstances and have totally different experiences. The difference was created by my own perceptions and the issues that resulted.

Probably the most significant relationship we begin and develop is the one with the person we choose for the most important, long term relationship of our lives. This person will become our life companion and in most cases, the other parent of our children. Our object is to build a life with that person. Our expectation is that they will be as supportive of us as we want to be of them. How can we make decisions during our dating years that will lead to making the best choice possible in our life mate? There is no magic formula for everyone but I will list a few suggestions from my own experience and observation that may help.

The first step is to make sure you are ready as a person. Think about where you are at in building relationships. Consider the relationship you have with your parents. Have you been able to develop an adult to adult relationship with them or do you allow them to treat you as a child? Perhaps when you go home, you revert to the child role and your parents are always encouraging you to grow up. Are you still looking for parental approval in all your decisions?

After relationships begin they are constantly developing and changing. The parent/child relationship needs to develop from care-giver/child to parent/friend which usually occurs during the teenage years as the young adult develops independence. The relationship can then progress to the adult/adult level.

Next, one needs to consider the relationship they have with their siblings. The only person we can change is ourselves. Only our input to a relationship is our responsibility. A good relationship with siblings or one with parents, for that matter, can only be achieved when both parties are willing to work at it. You can not change the way people choose to behave toward you, but you can change your reaction to it. What one has to consider is, "Do I allow anyone to affect me in a negative way?" If the answer is yes, you have some work to do on yourself. You want to be kind, loving, forgiving, understanding, considerate and compassionate without taking responsibility for the behaviors, choices and reactions of others.

When we are firstborn we are totally dependant on our parents for survival. As we get older, wise parents will have given us opportunities to mature in our ability to make choices for ourselves. Gradually we should have learned to make better and better choices and practiced skills for independence to the point that we can be totally self-sufficient. Teenagers naturally and constantly push for independence. It is a normal and natural part of the growing-up experience. That is when we gain confidence and prepare ourselves to go out on our own and take on the world. We need to get very confident at being independent before we can successfully learn the highest form of human interaction, which is inter-dependence. This stage of relationship development comes when two mature people come together, willing to support one another. They are able to do that without losing their own sense of self. They are then ready for a long-term relationship wherein each needs to have practiced independence until they no longer need anyone to look after them. They can make good choices that support them and are quite content and confident being on their own. They will then attract someone to them who has developed the same sort of independence and together they can develop that inter-dependence that is so necessary for a successful long term relationship.

When I began dating, I only went out with a few

young men and then at a very young age, began dating a man six years older than me. I ended up marrying while still a teenager. Because my mother died when I was only twelve years old, I think I was a little more mature than some of my peers. I certainly had learned life skills that equipped me for marriage, but I was in a fantasy land emotionally where I also believed in the "happily-ever-after" fairytale. I was lucky in that my marriage survived many years but believe me, it was pure luck.

I have observed that the evolution of relationships, and finally developing the ones that lead to finding your soul mate, can be compared to learning to shop for groceries.

Remember when you went grocery shopping for the first time? Perhaps it was when your mother sent you to the grocery store with a list. You wandered up and down the aisles with your shopping cart, trying to find the items with the specific brand names requested. You might have been given very clear instructions or had to rely on the experiences you had when your mother had taken you along. Chances are you made a few wrong choices and items had to be returned to the store or compensations were made and the items kept and used.

It may be that your first experience was when you left home, were in your own place and had to stock your cupboards for the first time. It could have been when you got a job so you could be independent, perhaps you went away to school, or got married. This time more choices had to be made because you had to rely on your own judgement. A much larger margin for error was open to you. You probably relied on the choices you were familiar with, the ones your mother or father had made, as you were growing up. The foods you learned to like as a child are the ones you will continue to prepare when you are on your own, simply because they were familiar to you. Most often we are drawn to that which we know and are comfortable with.

As time goes on you got more adventurous and seeing all the choices available, you gradually tried new foods, new recipes and expanded your tastes. As experiments were made, however, you probably noticed that your choices were influenced by culture and the cuisines from your first experiences with foods.

As we interrelate with people outside our family unit, we begin to identify traits that we are comfortable with, those we really like and admire and those we find difficult to accept or deal with. We begin to fill our mental shopping cart with ideas about what we really like, what we could tolerate and what we simply couldn't live with. We then become drawn to others who seem to have more of the traits on the 'really like' and 'could tolerate' lists, avoiding those who have more of the 'couldn't live with' traits. All the elements discussed previously in this chapter influence the categories in which we place these traits.

Getting to know a person's family can be very revealing. As observations are made during interactions with family members, many items can be added to your "trait" inventory and slotted under 'really like', 'could tolerate', or 'couldn't live with' categories. This process is very helpful when we are in the process of choosing people for long term relationships. The traits one first sees in another person are not necessarily who they are. Observing the person as they interact with their family will often uncover the reality.

When you feel mature enough to take on the responsibility of a partnership and you find someone who closely matches your shopping cart of traits, you become attracted to them. Then you begin to discover that you are someone who closely matches their choices of desired traits and the two of you come together naturally.

My first husband died just after we celebrated our forty-seventh wedding anniversary. I made up my mind that I had been there, done the marriage/parent thing and could be content with being a grandmother. I had even become very confident with being on my own. I could make decisions without consulting or getting the approval of anyone and was quite enjoying my new found freedom. Having worked on my childhood issues for twenty years, I was in a pretty good space. I had a sense of my own worth and was experiencing a full life - I thought.

At this juncture I became re-acquainted with a man I had known socially for about twenty-five years. My husband had passed away and as my friend put it; his marriage had died four years before. We went out as friends and began talking about what we would be looking for in a partner if we were to ever marry again. It wasn't long before the conversations went from, "if we got married," to "when we get married," to "planning the wedding!"

I am so glad I hit rock bottom all those years ago

and then spent the time working on my issues so that I could prepare myself for what I have now. As I worked on myself, I filled my own shopping cart with inventory that was harmonized with who I really was. I was then blessed with the opportunity to attract someone I could feel safe with and create a life filled with love and happiness.

We can't expect a life without challenges or a partner without a few imperfections that we need to learn to live with, but we should expect respect. It is only when we respect ourselves and then expect respect from others that we will get true respect.

Accepting our strengths as well as our limitations
is easier when we come from a solid self image.

CHAPTER THREE
WHO IS RESPONSIBLE?

Amy was feeling a little uneasy. This would be her
first day at playschool.

"I will stay with you as long as you need me," she
heard her mother say, but this was a new experience
for the little girl and she was always apprehensive in
new social situations.

Amy's blond hair was combed back and secured
by the fancy clips she loved to wear. She had insisted
on wearing her favorite pant and t-shirt outfit in her
favorite color. But then when she had expressed the
desire to take her Teddy-Bear, mom had persuaded

her to leave him home. "There will be many activities at playschool and Teddy will feel more comfortable at home while you're busy doing other things," mother had said.

This little blond-haired girl had been welcomed into the family by three older siblings. The whole family had adored her right from the start and she had been the focus of everyone's attention. During her first four years of life, love and acceptance had surrounded her. There were family members who lived close by and she had experienced many family gatherings playing with children younger and older than her.

The first day at playschool, Amy was welcomed by her teacher and the adults who helped out. The teacher introduced all the children to the play centers and Amy got excited as all the activities planned in the next few months were outlined. She tried one play center and then another and before long began to feel comfortable. When mom asked if it would be okay for her to leave now, Amy bravely said, "Yes." The rest of the morning went so fast, mom was there to pick her up before she realized it.

The next day Amy was up and ready well before it was time to go and she watched a little television to pass the time, then eagerly climbed in the car. When her mom pulled into the parking lot, Amy assured her mother that she could just drop her off. She liked play-school and was old enough to take care of herself, mother was informed.

During the morning's activities, Amy was pushed by a boy who got impatient for his turn. Later, when everyone was getting their outside clothes on to go home, the same boy grabbed one of her mittens and threatened to hide it. After a helper at the school intervened, Amy got her mitten and met her mom at the door. The situation with the boy seemed to get worse every day. The teacher and helpers tried to watch and correct the young man's behavior, but by the end of the week, when her mother asked how her day was, Amy blurted out, "Why doesn't Curtis like me?"

We have all experienced different forms of rejection, some of us very early in life. I am well aware that my early experiences influenced the way I met social situations. We all want to have friends and be a friend. As we approach a group of people the expectation is that we will be included. How well we are received and included can mean the difference between a good day and a bad one. How well we handle rejection can determine our happiness. If one has good self-worth it is easy to perceive that the way others treat them is more about the one who seems to be rejecting them. If one is functioning from a low self-worth, the tendency is to allow what is happening to reinforce any negative beliefs they have acquired regarding their own value.

As an adult, I have begun to analyze some of my behaviors and then tried to trace that behavior back to an experience through which I had accepted a negative belief. For example, I find it very difficult to "put myself out there," so to speak. I tend to avoid social situations where the possibility of rejection exists. Let's say I am going to a wedding reception by myself. I go through the receiving line and then look around the hall to find a table where no one is sitting. That is where I head with my plate of food and then accept others at my table as they come along.

One would think I was a very shy person, which is very far from the truth. I am very at home in front of a group of people, speaking, teaching, singing, conducting music or playing the piano. My difficulties come when I go one-on-one with others.

When I trace this behavior back, I again go to my early childhood, where I felt unaccepted by my mother. As a child I had a hard time making friends. I was alone much of the time. As an adolescent, I had one special friend for a few years, but again, I was alone as a teenager. My older sister on the other hand, as I stated in chapter two, was very social. She had two special friends and they were often referred to as the "Three Musketeers." I would often ask if I could be included and was always told, "You're too young."

Now as an adult I never expect to be included. I am at ease with planning dinner parties or events and inviting others to my home. I, however, will never go to someone else's home without an invitation. Not even to my children's homes. On the few occasions when I dare to suggest I meet a friend somewhere and there is even a hint of reluctance on their part, I back down and isolate myself. It is a self protection mechanism. If I go to an event and feel the least bit unwelcome, I remove myself from the situation. This is my issue and I am learning to deal with it better. I can't expect others to make a social life for me. I know I have missed out on many good opportunities to meet new people and make new friends in the past and I have come a long way toward being a social person. I now tend to give others the benefit of the doubt. There are many people out there just like I was. I am more and more becoming the one who takes the first step in befriending them. I need to re-emphasize here:

A negative experience usually creates a negative belief. That belief becomes the base from which we function ever after.

Unless the belief is identified and an effort made to change, it becomes very difficult to function in a more positive way.

Because cognitive reasoning begins to develop around age four, continuing to around age twelve, many perceptions that children form before and during cognitive reasoning development often become negative beliefs that can affect self-esteem. A person's beliefs are their reality. That is why choices, reactions and behaviors are influenced thereafter. Children may come to conclusions that may be out of harmony with what was intended simply because the child is unequipped with the reasoning powers to understand the motives and reasons for choices being made by others.

Of course all parents, concerned about the well-being of their children, do all they can to demonstrate love and caring for each of them. They recognize that building self-esteem can help children feel their own worth and do everything possible, within their knowledge and power, to instil it. Ideally the responsibility to emotionally support one's self is learned and taken on. Supporting one's self from within, rather than looking to outside sources, is the most desirable outcome.

Self-esteem issues can undermine our self confidence and cause us to question our capabilities. These issues create stress because we have to constantly push ourselves to explore, experiment and satisfy our curiosity. These are all important elements of our learning process. Feeling safe to make mistakes, learn from them and try again, is essential to the learning process as well.

I worked with a man in his early forties who was suffering from migraine headaches. Dan was successful in his career as a physical education teacher in a high school. All the young people he worked with admired and respected him and he was a great father. On the surface, this man seemed to have it all, but every two weeks, as regular as clock work he would have to spend a weekend in bed full of pain killers and with the room darkened. Sometimes it would get so bad that a sick day would have to be used to cope with his problem.

As we worked together, every possible physical cause of migraine headaches was explored. Then we began looking for emotional causes and discovered that he had been struggling with a safety issue all his life. Safety issues can be very complex and we finally narrowed it down to his feeling unsafe to build relationships. A negative belief was acquired out of a negative experience he had around age three.

There had been a family picnic planned. A nice spot was selected by a little creek, where a bonfire could be started. The family had enjoyed roasting wieners and finally the fire had died down so that marshmallows could be placed on sticks and held over the live coals. The marshmallows were then browned and would be crispy on the outside but yet warm and soft on the inside. It was a pleasant summer evening and twilight lingered long enough so that the children could explore the natural woods by the creek.

The bonfire had died down so that the live coals were covered with white ash and little Dan thought it would be nice to run through the soft ashes in his bare feet. He was unaware that beneath the white ash were hot coals. Sitting down, he removed his shoes and socks and implemented his plan before any of the adults could get to him and intervene. The bottoms of his feet were badly burned. From this experience he perceived that he could no longer trust his caregivers to keep him safe, that his whole world was unsafe and he needed to be on guard all the time in order to protect himself. If he couldn't trust others, it wasn't safe to build relationships. Operating from these negative beliefs, from then on, he had to be pushed into social situations. As an adolescent he held himself back, afraid to get involved. Gradually he learned to push himself but was always guarded and cautious. The stress it had created over the years resulted in physical symptoms. Working on the safety issues relieved the stress and the migraine headaches gradually disappeared.

An old experience that undermines our self-esteem can be triggered by the subconscious, sometimes when we least expect it, causing us to lose our self-confidence in a present situation.

Stephanie was a bright ambitious girl who, after graduating from high school, had received her degree in journalism and was now the top executive for a well known women's magazine. However, six months into her new position she realized that help was needed. Many successes had been hers but every time she called the staff into the board room for a meeting, she was still experiencing nausea and cold sweats. Sure that her staff could sense the insecurity she felt and could hear her knees knocking together, she took steps to get some assistance in understanding her re-action to the situation.

It was discovered that the source of her problem was a negative experience she had at the age of ten. She was visiting her grandfather's farm and she and her cousin were playing with matches near the gas drums. The grass caught on fire and of course mom, dad, grandpa, grandma and an uncle came running from the house. The fire was out in minutes but years later the memory of the well-deserved tongue lash-ing that followed was triggered in her subconscious every time she got in a situation where all eyes in the room were on her. This caused her to lose all her confidence and she couldn't even think of the words needed to express herself.

The last chapter dealt with many elements that can affect our ability to build relationships and how the in-teraction in relationships can affect the development of self-esteem. Feeling safe in the world and know-ing that we belong here is the foundation of self-es-teem. Our state of being is the first step to building a good sense of self. When we are secure in the first step, it is easy for us to explore and experiment. We participate in life and discover our capabilities. The ability to think for ourselves is the next step and then comes the development of our own identity, enabling the discovery of the power within us. Next we learn that there is a social structure that we need to operate within and that others have boundaries we need to respect. We then begin to realize that we have the right to have our own boundaries. The discovery of our own identity which includes our sexuality helps us to begin learning that we are able to function separate from our parents and siblings and is a necessary step in developing our own independence.

Considering the questions listed below that identify many aspects of self-esteem may be helpful to parents who are concerned about what they might do to support its development as they rear their children. It will also provide a check list for those who are wondering whether they are mature enough and ready to take responsibility for themselves independent of their caregivers. For many it can be used for self examination where ever you presently are in life.

QUESTIONS FOR SELF EXAMINATION:

1. Do you feel your world is safe, that you belong here and are glad to be alive?
2. Do you feel confident that all your needs will be taken care of, that you have the skills to take care of yourself at your level of physical and mental development, and that you have the ability to learn all you will need to for completely taking that responsibility?
3. Are you able to honestly say you love yourself? Do you accept who you are and where you are in

your growth process allowing yourself to develop at your own pace?

4. Are you able to participate comfortably in inter-relations with others and feel acceptance as you grow, improve and change?

5. Do you feel comfortable with all your feelings both negative (anger, fear, guilt, sadness) and positive (joy, excitement, peace, satisfaction)? Do you feel safe and comfortable expressing your feelings and are you able to do that in appropriate ways while being respectful of others and sensitive to their situations?

6. Are you able to acknowledge that every person demonstrates love in their own unique way and can you accept love from others in the way that *they* are most comfortable expressing it?

7. Do you internalize only love, support and respect from others and are you able to screen out the negativity of others, recognizing when they are acting out of their own issues and give them re-sponsibility for their reactions and behaviors?

8. Are you able to accept criticism as an offer for help and only treat it as information for you to consider?

9. Do you accept the judgements of others simply as statements about the level they are at in their own growth experience?

10. Do you feel that you have to do everything by yourself or do you recognize that you have a sup-port system around you?

11. Are you patient with yourself and able to prac-tice in order to learn new skills?

12. Are you able to acknowledge your own capabilities and have confidence in your ability to contribute in ways that are satisfying to you?

13. Are you flexible and willing to expand your world, easily adapting to new situations, and implement new ideas and information?

14. Do you feel that you are loved whether you are being productive or taking time to relax?

15. Are you able to take responsibility for every thought, feeling and behavior that you choose and recognize that you need only take responsibility for your input or contribution to situations?

16. Do you recognize that anger is simply a message from your emotional self that you or someone you care about has experienced an injustice and then take the steps to stand up to the offender in ways that respect their rights while defending yours?

17. Is it easy for you to say no when you need to set up boundaries or defend yourself? Can you say no in a way that honors the rights of others?

18. Do you feel safe in learning situations and can you easily take time to think things through?

19. Are you able give others time and space to do their thinking without feeling you need to jump in and think for them or give them help when it would be best for them to work it out for themselves?

20. Are you able to ask for help when you need it? When you ask for help do you continue to feel that you are powerful, capable and intelligent?

21. Can you be by yourself or work with others and feel secure in both situations?

22. Do you feel loved when you are alone as well as when you are with others?

23. Are you comfortable with being unique and able to celebrate the successes of others as well as your own?

24. Can you ask others about themselves and still feel your own value?

25. Have you learned that positive behavior brings positive results and that most often negative behavior will bring negative results? Are you able to change your behavior to get the results that you want?

26. Are you able to respond appropriately to what is real and that which is pretend?

27. Do you acknowledge that it is acceptable to just be yourself?

28. Do you think and reason before you speak?

29. Are you decisive and able to make decisions easily following through on action that supports that decision? Do you acknowledge that it is acceptable to change your mind with the addition of new information or circumstances?

30. Are you able to allow others to make their own decisions?

31. Do you understand that rules are needed to ensure safety and fairness for everyone?

32. Can you accept that rules are important guidelines for you to follow enabling you to contribute to the positive living of yourself and others?

33. Do you feel confident in your own opinions and yet are able to accept that others have a right to theirs? Are you able to give others respect when expressing their opinions and yet able to disagree with confidence in your own convictions?

34. Do you feel loved by others and continue to love yourself even when you make mistakes or disagree as you interrelate?

35. Are you comfortable with your own sexuality and the roles (son/daughter, brother/sister, husband/wife, father/mother, etc.) that are determined by your sexuality?

36. Do you live independently according to your level of skill, ability and knowledge and are willing to learn, practice and implement more advance skills taking responsibility to fill your own needs?

37. Are you able to nurture yourself sufficient for your own needs?

A "yes" answer indicates positive beliefs in areas that support good self-esteem. A "no" answer should invite investigation in order to identify the negative belief that might be operating. All can benefit from examining and letting go of that which undermines a healthy self image and taking steps to introduce positive beliefs that are more supportive. Change can then take place.

There are five aspects to our mind body system:

- **physical**
- **intellectual**
- **emotional**

- **social**

- **and spiritual**

All five aspects need attention and consideration if we are to develop and maintain good self-esteem. Self-image should develop to the point that our own acceptance is all we really need and we are solid in our self chosen standards, beliefs and values. When we are at this point, rejection from others can be easily managed. We allow others to own their own issues and are able to be the kind of person we want to be. In my experience, most people want to be kind, loving, forgiving, understanding, compassionate and supportive. When negative behaviors hold us back from being the kind of person we want to be, it is an indication that we are acting out of negative beliefs that we automatically respond to instead of positive ones where a positive reaction or action is automatic. How often have you thought back to a situation and wished you would have reacted differently? Chances are you have vowed that you would respond differently the next time but when the opportunity presents itself again, you react in the same old way.

Often we find ourselves taking responsibility for others. This becomes a no-win situation. First we give away our power and secondly, others are weakened when they are continually rescued and someone else takes on their challenges as their own. Sometimes the best help you can give others is no help at all. When our self-esteem is healthy it is easy to discern the line between when giving support with actual physical assistance or when only encouragement, suggestions and or emotional support are best. It takes a strong person to allow someone they love to struggle, even when it is best for them.

Our physical system includes our physical appearance, our physical functions and our sexuality. How we perceive each of these elements in ourselves can affect self-esteem. If you look in the mirror and have negative feelings about the reflection looking back at you, then you would benefit from taking responsibility for accepting what you see or taking steps to improve the image you see. When people believe that they are not worth caring for, it is difficult to take the time needed to nurture themselves in any way. Everything else is more important; more important than proper food and nutrition, keeping physically fit, practicing good grooming habits, or learning and developing a sense of style enabling one to buy, choose and wear clothing that enhances physical appearance and is appropriate for every social situation.

Many times I have worked with people, especially teenagers, who have developed issues around their physical appearance. They have become so stressed out over it that physical symptoms such as stomach or bowel problems have occurred. Peer acceptance can be a very big issue for young people and physical appearance is often attacked.

I began to develop very young. By the time I was eleven years old, my breasts were bigger than any of the other girls my age and most of the older girls as well. Many of the boys began teasing me and I became the target of name calling. "Buckets" and "Gasobs" were some of their favorites. Needless to say I became very self conscious and tried everything I could to camouflage my developing figure. The damage done to my self-esteem took years to recover from.

Physical functions are not only connected to how our body moves, but physical conditions we have become challenged with as well as female and male processes connected with sexuality. Some of us are healthy and well coordinated. Some view themselves as clumsy, while others struggle with physical challenges of various kinds. Issues with our own sexuality are common.

When I was young, I was uncoordinated. When sides were chosen for a baseball game, I was among the last to be chosen. I remember going to the school yard every night for two weeks with a girlfriend. She patiently ran for the volleyball time after time, retrieving it as I practiced. This was just so I could get the ball across the net when it was my turn to serve and keep it somewhere in the court.

Finally I decided that reading was much more rewarding and I became a bookworm, and an honor student, or in today's terms, a "nerd." I would claim I had no interest in athletics, but deep inside I was hurting because athletes were also the popular kids in school. Accepting our strengths as well as our limitations is easier if we come from a solid self-image.

Our sexuality is a very big part of who we are. If we are born male, we are first a son. If we have siblings or acquire them, we are a brother. We can be a husband, father and uncle. Females take on the role of daughter, sister and can be a wife, mother and aunt. Being unable to accept our sexuality greatly undermines our sense of who we are.

Any form of abuse, physical, emotional and/or sexual is very detrimental to self-esteem. Usually physical and sexual abuse is accompanied by emotional abuse, and the abuser, in order to justify the action, will attempt to convince the abused that he or she is responsible. Sexual abuse, in my opinion, is the most damaging. It tears at the very heart of who we are and can cause us to become confused about our sexual identity. People of both sexes and all ages are affected by it in today's society. The abuse ranges all the way from verbal, to inappropriate touching, to penetration. The verbal abuse can include any communication that attacks sexuality with the intention of causing the other person to feel shame around being male or female or in regards to any of their body parts. Any inappropriate interaction of a sexual nature through enticement, coercion or force is abuse and becomes a negative sexual experience. When it happens to a child, before they are mature enough to fully understand or manage it, their self-esteem is severely damaged and much healing is required in order to move past the experience. Some negative beliefs acquired might be:

- I am unsafe being a male (or female).
- I must feel shame about my body and its functions or when I have sexual feelings.
- I must punish myself for being male (or female).
- I am a bad person now and undeserving of respect, love or acceptance.
- My body has been used and is no longer special.
- I must give others control over me, my life and my body.

The intellectual system is connected to our own intelligence and our ability to learn. Often parents will compare one child to another, thinking this will acknowledge success on one hand and provide the motivation to measure up on the other. Most often it only tears down self-esteem.

Sometimes comparing is first experienced in school when we first notice that Suzy is "getting it" and I am not. Often then, the deduction is made that she is smart and I am dumb. This continues throughout our experience in the education system as classifications of average, above or below average are made in an endeavor to measure where, in the opinion of the instructors, we are at. Often, in an effort to help, labels are given to some students. That is when we begin to measure our own intellectual abilities through the opinions of others and compare ourselves to those around us. Unfortunately we seem to look to those whom we feel are more successful than we are, and in our eyes, always come up short.

Our emotional system relates to our ability to feel, process and express all our emotions. Often we have been taught to "stuff our emotions" because people around us know how to be with us when we are expressing positive feelings and are uncomfortable when it is clear that we are feeling negative emotion. Think how often we hear, "little boys don't cry", or "bad girl". Often we are told we are bad when we have expressed anger in an inappropriate way. Feelings don't make us good or bad, and feelings in and of themselves are not good or bad, they are just feelings. How we express those feelings may be good or bad depending on how we choose to express ourselves and whether or not we have been disrespectful of people or their boundaries and rights. If however, we have accepted that we are good when we have good feelings, and bad when we feel negative emotion, we will learn to "stuff" our negative feelings instead of learning to process them in ways that help us analyze the situation. We are unable, then, to discover what caused us to experience the feeling and determine how we need to take care of ourselves emotionally in order to make things right in our world.

It is great to feel happy, enthused, elated, surprised, ecstatic, joyful, content, cheerful, fortunate, prosperous and all other positive ways that ensure us that all is right in our world. When we feel sad, bored, apathetic, depressed, physical or emotional pain, unsatisfied, gloomy, victimized, deprived or any other negative way, it is a message to us that something needs to be taken care of. The often used method is medication, and frequently it is needed in order to get us through an initial bout of anxiety, depression, or physical pain. Eventually though, getting to the core of the problem and learning to process our emotions in healthy ways is the best solution.

Social systems include all our relationships and our ability to interact with everyone we include in our family circle and extended family. We learned in the last chapter how healthy inner circle relationships give us the confidence to reach out to include friends and the relationship with our significant other. Identifying negative beliefs and patterns within ourselves can help us to understand our own choices and behaviors and help us to change those things that are not getting us what we want in life.

Everyone has a spiritual aspect within themselves that needs attention as well. We all need to feel that there is a higher power than us that we can reach out to and connect with when all within us seems exhausted. We may choose to call it, the power of the universe, the higher power within us, Buddha, Mohamad, God or something else. Some feel that the only spiritual people out there are those who are belong to an organized religion and go to church every Sunday. It has been my experience that there are many spiritual people who never darken the door of a church, and there are many people who attend church every week, who go there for the wrong reasons but are not necessarily spiritual.

Our spirituality should give us an inner assurance that we are each unique and special. We each have gifts, talents and attributes that give us value and worth. Each of us deserves consideration and respect. We are all worthy and deserving of love, acceptance and support and particularly worthy and deserving of our share of the earth's abundance. Above all, each of us is worthy of support from what ever we believe is the source of our spiritual power.

When we have a self-esteem that supports us, rejection from others cannot undermine it. We can be humble and teachable, accept criticism and judgement as information that we need to consider, and choose to accept that which would help us move forward. The strength within us to take care of our own emotional needs will be there. Self-recognition and acceptance will be ours, and competing with ourselves and our endeavor to improve on our last performance, will be good enough. We will recognize that we not only have the right, but the obligation to develop our own beliefs, standards and values, based on our own experiences. We may accept the beliefs, standards and values of others, such as our parents, because we have examined them, and found them to be in harmony with that which supports us, but can feel confident that it is acceptable to recognize and take on beliefs and patterns that move us in more positive directions.

Honoring our own integrity will be our priority and what comes from within will be more important than what comes at us from outside ourselves. We can be ourselves and know that who we are is enough. We will no longer be intimidated by the critics of the world and be unconcerned about whether they like us or not. Respect from others will be more important. Our social expectations will be realistic in that we will understand that everyone has their own issues and may not be able to relate to us in our preferred way. We will be self-confident and feel comfortable and capable in all social situations. Each person only needs to be responsible for their own behaviors, reactions, beliefs, opinions and inputs or contributions. It is important to take that responsibility and then recognize that we have the power to change whatever we dislike about what we see in ourselves. Often as we make changes in ourselves the reactions and actions of others toward us will change.

When we love and accept ourselves
at each stage of our growth process
we are able to give ourselves and others
the time and space we all need to grow and learn.

CHAPTER FOUR
NOW THAT'S A BALANCE

Do you know someone who just can't get going?
Everyone they know sees great potential in them, but
they just can't see it in themselves. Their negative self-
talk is expressed vocally and you are sure that it goes
on in their head when they are unable to find an audience. Although they have summoned the nerve to try
various things, their endeavors seem to fail more often
than the average person.

Matt had become a couch potato, but now prefers

to identify himself as the one whose responsibility it is, "to hold the couch down." Over the years, he had gained various employment opportunities, but quit because the boss was too controlling, his co-workers expected him to do all the work, the job wasn't challenging enough, he wanted to spend his time doing something that would support his goals, but there was always a problem: Matt really had no goals.

His day begins at around 10 a.m. when Matt gets up and into the shower in order to wake himself up. He gets morning paper, turns to the "Help Wanted" ads and skims through them as he gets a bite to eat. His wife left hours ago after getting the kids off to school and herself to her place of employment.

A few phone calls are made following up job possibilities (he has to tell Nancy, his wife, that he had put some time into the search when she gets home). A little rest is needed before he can do one of the jobs Nancy outlined for him to get done that day. Late afternoon is usually spent with Oprah and Dr. Phil. He sometimes starts dinner and helps a little when Nancy and the kids get home and then he parks himself in front of the television, turns to the sports channel and watches until past midnight when he finally turns into bed.

People who have checked out of life to this extreme come in both sexes and all shapes and sizes. Some are highly intelligent and some are challenged in their ability to learn, but all have usually given in to either a fear of success or a fear of failure.

The fear of failure is easily understood by all. It is easy to see that if a person has had many failure experiences they are simply afraid to try again, but a fear of success is sometimes hard to comprehend. After all, aren't we all striving for success?

The fear of success usually comes from trying to live up to the expectations of others and feeling you're never going to measure up. Soon it is easier to just keep falling short in an endeavor to force the relaxation of expectations. Think about what happens when we do well at something. Everyone expects us to continue to repeat the performance time after time. If we fail to measure up, people say, "What happened to you?" They are clearly disappointed in us. When we feel the disappointment we often interpret it as a form of rejection.

Now think back to your school experience. Right from the first grade, as soon as we completed a task and the teacher saw that we were finished another task was given out, so we never really finished. If a student is someone who enjoys completing tasks, that becomes a motivator. If the student feels overwhelmed by all the work, soon the only answer is to reduce the performance and in doing so diminish the expectations from parents and teachers. This learned behavior can easily be continued into adulthood.

In my experience it all stems from a negative belief, "I am without the right to set my own expectations of myself and I must allow someone else to do it for me. It is my job to measure up to those expectations." Changes in behavior can only be made if one can change the beliefs to:

- I am in charge of my life.
- I have the right to set my own expectations of myself.

- I have the obligation to myself to set realistic expectations.
- When ever I fall short of my self expectations, I forgive myself and try again.
- I am intelligent and capable.
- I have the ability to learn and develop new skills.
- I only need to compete with myself and improve on my last performance.

Then the person can participate in life more fully creating the success that is really desired. I have never known a person who is happy with him or herself when they are in a pattern of non-achievement.

What about the people who are always after the "pie in the sky". It is difficult for them to have a regular job and work for someone else, yet they are unable to create success being self-employed. They try one thing after another and every attempt goes sour. Confident that their next project will bring them the fortune and fame they are seeking they attempt one thing after another. Sometimes able to convince others that their next scheme will work, and occasionally they even drag others down with them. They are constantly living with anxiety, although they would be the first to deny it. Outwardly they exude confidence and appear to be self-assured.

There are several negative beliefs that could be motivating this behavior. Probably the dominant one is, "I can only get acceptance when I am wealthy and influential by the world's standards." Usually the people who brag about their successes or have a need to take the biggest risks, have the lowest self-esteem and try to compensate for it through constantly attempting to prove to themselves and others that they have what it takes to be successful. The problem is the measure of their success lies in wealth and influence.

As always, the negative beliefs first need to be discovered before changes can be made. It often helps to investigate self-esteem and choices made to replace the negative with beliefs that support instead of diminish. An examination of one's definition of abundance will reveal whether it is just connected to money and prestige or the main focus is love, respect, healthy relationships, contentment, peace and other elements that contribute to feelings of security. Satisfying success comes when all outcomes are perceived as positive. Even when the result achieved falls short of expectations, if mistakes were used as learning experiences, new plans can be made and the motivation to try again maintained.

I'm sure you have experienced or know people who are visibly anxious, frustrated and always on the go. You are tempted to say, "Chill out! Hang Loose! Take it easy!" Why can't these people do that? What is holding them back? Why must they take on anything and everything, scheduling every minute of every day until time for them becomes nothing but a long forgotten dream? Let's observe Ellen, and perhaps we can find some answers.

Her alarm goes off at 5 a.m. She must get up and start her day as everything depends on her. She tidies the house, folds the laundry and lays out clothing for each member of the family. At 6:30 a.m. she wakes up the children to get them going. Ellen steps into the shower and hurriedly moves through her grooming ritual.

Checking to see how the children are coming along is next on the schedule and soon, sounds of lunch and breakfast preparation can be heard coming from the kitchen. Family breakfast is served promptly at 7 a.m. every morning, so Scott, her husband, can leave for work by 7:30. Ellen and the children must be out the door by 8:30. The children catch a school bus and Ellen drives to a part-time job that keeps her until 2 p.m. every day. It never fails, that last hour in the morning is filled with the unexpected - homework that needs to be finished; organizing materials for a school project one of the children had forgotten to mention earlier; a basketball uniform that is still wet in the washer and needs to be power dried. Reminders must be given to each child to brush their teeth, tidy their rooms or organize their backpack and, "Don't forget your lunch".

Once her little brood is out the door, she moves through the house, inspecting every room to make sure it looks perfect. She detests coming home from work and seeing anything out of order. Finally in the car, providing the last house check didn't take too long and if it isn't snowing or raining, causing traffic problems, the drive to work gives a needed break. But most days she sits in traffic, worrying about being late and is constantly being irritated by inconsiderate drivers, who in her mind, are out to get her.

Work is dealing with disgruntled customers and complaints. She must be polite, understanding and yet firm with company policy. It is an unrewarding job that drains her. The dream of the career she really wanted to pursue, has long since been put on her 'maybe some day' list. But the money she generates is needed to support all the children in their sports, dancing, art and speech classes, gymnastics, wood working and music programs.

Home by 2:30 or 3:00 p.m., she takes a few minutes to organize dinner and then she is ready to chauffeur the children to their games or practices, lessons or rehearsals. Ellen drops the kids off and is sometimes able to shop for groceries or pick up materials needed for up-coming projects or costumes. Occasionally she returns library books or picks up music needed for lessons.

Back home, dinner preparations are completed. The meal must be on the table, ready to eat at 6 p.m. sharp. Ellen organizes the children with their home-work assignments and then cleans up after dinner. She had tried getting the family involved once but every job had to be done over in order to get it right.

Tutoring and helping with assignments and projects is the next order of the day. Sometimes she can work on a dance costume at the same time. Once bed-time stories are read and the children are tucked in for the night, planning for the next day demands her attention.

Finally, exhausted, Ellen climbs into bed, but can't get to sleep because of the dialogue going on in her head. *"I need to be a better mom, I snapped at Chad today. It wasn't his fault. The kids must think I'm a witch. If only I could do things faster and better. Why do I feel so drained all the time? Maybe I need vita-*

mins. I just need to get more organized. All the other moms seem to be able to handle it. What's wrong with me? Susan works full-time and never seems to get rattled. I'm such a failure."

There is no relief on weekends. The routine may change slightly but every minute is scheduled. There is time for everyone except Ellen. She gets no breaks, no relief, no time off, and it's beginning to feel like no thanks.

Analyzing Ellen's life, it is easy to see that she is a perfectionist and needs to share some responsibilities with others in her family. She is obsessed with her mother role and takes on anything and everything. Self-criticism dominates her thoughts and she is overly concerned about what others think.

What are some negative beliefs that Ellen could be accommodating? Usually a belief that acceptance is based on performance underlies a perfectionist trait. Because acceptance is one of the five basic emotional needs, it almost becomes a matter of life and death to perform well. Ellen probably knows that delegating responsibilities to each member of the family provides opportunities to learn life skills. It would help them feel they are an important part of a unit and give each a sense of belonging. She knows that accepting what others are capable of while providing encouragement and offering guidance, and giving each one space to grow and learn is important. But perfectionists find it hard to be flexible and if Ellen can't love and forgive herself, it is difficult for her to really love and forgive others.

An examination of Ellen's motivation behind involving the children in so many extra-curricular activities would be helpful. This would assist her in setting priorities that would create a balance between the personal quality-time each child needs from her, and providing opportunities for them to pursue their interests. Is Ellen providing them because the children want and need them? Or does it make her look good as a parent? Children need many experiences as they grow and learn, but do they need them all at once? Children need, above all, love and security.

If Ellen has learned that taking time for her is selfish, she needs to understand that taking that time would make her stronger and more balanced. When a person is more balanced and centered they make better decisions and are more patient. They give to others because they want to, rather that feeling like they have to.

In reality, acceptance should be unconditional. What we do may be unacceptable but acceptance of each individual should be unconditional. Embracing certain truths can overcome the negativity.

1. If you value and respect yourself, others will value and respect you.

2. If you take your turn, others will recognize that you deserve your turn.

3. If you set boundaries and create balance in your life by receiving as much as you give, you model one of the most important principles you can teach to your family and others.

As each of the five systems (physical, emotional, intellectual, social and spiritual) discussed in chapter three are examined and considered, every individual can identify issues that need to be resolved. When issues are addressed, self-value increases. Sometimes it is just a matter of becoming aware and then making a conscious effort to change our thinking. Lives are created through decisions. Self-value influences decisions. People who believe that their value and acceptance are based on performance, or the material wealth they acquire, usually put pressure on themselves and sometimes on others through unrealistic expectations. They often become perfectionists and workaholics. Sometimes their unrealistic expectations are made solely on circumstances and they make decisions without fully researching all aspects of a project or venture. Blame gets placed on circumstances or other people for undesired results. Those who check out completely, usually place responsibility outside themselves as well.

In order to change the results, behavior needs to change. In order to change behavior, each person needs to take responsibility for their own issues and make the effort to change their thinking through identifying negative beliefs.

When some or all of the five systems have gone un-nourished, self protection is needed for survival. Because the intentions of others can only be perceived, often a decision is made on how we need to interact and protect ourselves, based on false information. As discussed in a previous chapter, when a decision is made on false information it becomes a negative belief. Once a negative belief has been accepted it must be accommodated through the decisions we make.

The only person we have the right or the power to change is ourselves. Part of understanding ourselves is understanding our personality type:

a) Someone who processes everything mentally and is very analytical. Most often this type is a good leader and verbal communicator.

b) The intuitive, sensitive type uses touch as they communicate.

c) Someone who is spontaneous and expresses feelings easily. This type usually communicates with hand gestures.

d) There are radical types who are motivated and creative but unpredictable.

Being aware that there are many personality types, discovering yours and learning to develop yourself in harmony with that type helps you to not only appreciate the many attributes that your type gives you, but what needs to be learned in order for you to move forward in the best way.

When I began to heal from my depression, I first needed to recognize that many personality types were represented in all the people I interacted with. I made the mistake of expecting everyone to know what I had learned, what I believed and see everything the way I did. My understanding of all the types helped me to accept others as they were and accept the way they expressed their own personality. I was then able to accept myself as I was. It helped me to understand that I was the type of person who puts all their heart, soul, focus and energy into a project, spends all their energy and then crashes - a sprinter as opposed to a distance runner. I used to feel guilty about having a power nap during the day. I even thought there was something wrong with me. As a result I would power out about noon and then push myself to make it through the rest of the day. I now know that taking time out is the best thing I can do for myself but also for others around me, because doing so makes me easier to live with.

I have discovered that many people believe that they are being selfish if they take time for themselves. In reality a person is very unselfish if they do. Identifying how we need to nurture ourselves and support our self-esteem gives us the power and ability to be better people and give what is necessary in developing all our relationships. When we love and accept ourselves at each stage of our growth process we are able to give ourselves and others the time and space needed to grow and learn. Taking care of ourselves teaches our children and others that each person needs to take responsibility in caring for themselves. Caring for ourselves enables us to make better choices. We can better discern whether the best choice is to rescue others or to allow them to learn on their own. Time is managed more efficiently and attention given to what matters most. We begin to give unconditionally and do the right things for the right reasons. As people learn to value themselves, they become more sensitive to ways others need to be nurtured in each of the five areas. The cycle of unrealistic expectations made of self and others can be broken. Life becomes balanced, relaxed and enjoyable.

We can get to the point where our self-confidence

can move us forward and we can create positive out-comes for ourselves in all we attempt, free of the need to compete. We are more likely to fully research the pros and cons in each situation before choosing to take a risk. We can begin to use time in a way that gives adequate attention to our daily work, play, relax-ation and rest, developing meaningful relationships, and increasing our abilities, talents and knowledge.

Now that's balance!

CHAPTER FIVE
ON LIVING HAPPILY EVER AFTER

When a story begins 'Once upon a time,' everyone expects what follows to be either fiction or fantasy. However, many people still anticipate after a wedding 'they lived happily ever after' will automatically come next. All of the seasoned veterans of marriage are much more realistic. Most of our life's lessons come from interaction with other human beings. It is from our relationships that we learn to share, develop understanding and compassion, learn to make concessions, to lead or follow, respect others, and practice forgiveness.

It is true that opposites attract. We are usually drawn to others for relationships, because of the ways we are different as much as what we have in common. Each person has their comfort zone developed from childhood experiences. What we are used to is "normal" for us. Each family has its own patterns and these patterns establish what will be viewed as normal by each individual in that family.

Two people from two different family patterns, with two different ideas of what normal is and each having different needs, are drawn to each other. A relationship develops. Each sees in the other qualities they are attracted to and think they want in a companion. Even though they only have limited experience with each other and life in general, they decide to get married. Each expects the same consideration they were given by the other during the courtship to continue after marriage.

As time goes on, the stresses of daily living cause certain characteristics to emerge that were not evident during the time their relationship was more relaxed. Disappointment sets in when they realize there is a vast difference between what they expected and what is happening. How each partner is able to handle the difference determines the success of the marriage.

Experience shows one of the biggest challenges in marriage is creating a new pattern out of the two established during each partner's individual childhood. When one partner is expected to give up their own comfort zone and accept or adapt to that which is only familiar to the other partner, difficulties start arising. They may be more than the deprived partner can handle.

In chapter two a concept was discussed indicating that it is ideal for each partner to develop the ability for inter-dependence. Newborn babies are totally dependant but as we grow, total independence is usually gradually developed. This becomes very evident during the teenage years. Finally, as we mature, experience is gained in interrelating with others and the potential for inter-dependence develops. Ideally, each individual is then strong enough for independence if necessary, but can also share, respect another's space, care enough about someone else to be concerned about their needs, and make concessions, but be strong enough to set boundaries so their own needs are respected.

There are several elements that are needed in any successful long-term relationship. The most important is each person having the capacity to love. From that love, acceptance and accommodation of differences, openness, respect, communication and willingness to forgive usually develop.

Because I married very young, I was also very inexperienced in male/female relationships. I had acquired most of the life skills I needed because of the responsibility I had to take on after my mother died. I was, however, a bit of a loner while growing up and so I lacked social skills. Because I was void of close friends, when I received attention from a young man six years my senior, I was flattered to say the least. He was kind to me and became the friend I never had, so I became very attached and grateful for the attention. We dated for a couple of years and made plans to be married. My father was pretty much in his own world, having lost his partner and because my mother was young when they were married, he was open to our engagement.

We were married and lived in a little two-roomed house that we had moved onto a piece of land my dad gave us for a wedding present. My husband, David, worked as a trucker and was gone four days a week. The three days he was home, we worked on our little home, and spent time with our families and friends. The first real problem came with David's interest in model airplanes. I got pregnant very early in our marriage and was about six months along when spring came and he began spending his days off at the schoolyard where he and his airplane buddies spent their time. I came from a family where meals were always on time. My dad was a mechanic and had regular hours at his shop. Even after Mom passed away, my sister and I were expected to prepare the meals and have them ready to serve when Dad came home.

My husband's family were farmers. They got up in the morning, went to the barn, took care of animals and milked the cows before breakfast was served. Often his mom would get side-tracked with household chores or gardening and was only reminded that a meal was needed when everyone was standing around the table wondering what there was to eat. Regularly, the older children would just cook eggs and slice bread for the younger ones as mom would still be occupied with what ever took her attention.

Much of the time, even though the dinner hour was announced early in the day, the family would come in at the scheduled time and the meal wasn't even started. So when I told David that dinner would be at a certain time, he expected that he could be late without a problem. I tried discussing my idea of promptness, and the importance to me of having his respect, but with no improvement. Finally one day after keeping dinner warm for a couple of hours, when he finally arrived, I told him he obviously didn't want dinner and I scraped his plate in to the garbage. I got tired of waiting and had eaten earlier. I'm not sure that was the best choice but I finally got his attention.

There was also a little problem over my husband commenting, "Mom doesn't cook it like that," or "Mom always made it this way". He got his dinner scraped into the garbage another time with my reply, "Maybe you should go and eat with your mom." Well it worked for the other problem, why not this one?

When our first child was born, David became very resentful of this little person who was taking my time and attention. He was the oldest boy in a family of seven children. His dad had struggled with poor health from the time my husband could remember and so from a very young age, much of the responsibility in running the farm as well as sharing parental responsibilities had been placed on his shoulders. Feeling that he had already raised a family he wasn't excited to be a father so soon in our marriage and he certainly didn't want a big family. I finally talked him into having a second child when our first was nearly two years old, but the reluctance to really participate in parenting was always there.

We moved from the farm to the city when our oldest daughter was four years old. Through the previous four years we had struggled financially. My husband was laid off from the trucking job, and then we moved onto his parents' farm to help out when his dad had a stroke. The family farm was sold and we moved in with his parents for a time when they bought a restaurant. The idea was to help them until they regained their health and financial stability. Finally David went to work for a rancher in the area and then we decided that the only way we were going to get ahead was to get away from farming.

In the city, it became necessary for me to get a job as well. It was very hard to leave my children and turn their care over to someone else but financially, there was no other choice. It took two minimum wage jobs to pay the bills and we certainly couldn't afford to drive the car much. There were many discussions over budgets and finances and many disagreements about priorities. At least we had learned to listen to each other and were able to resolve our issues for the most part.

I recognize now that I had a weakness that eventually caused a big problem in our marriage. I had a hard time standing my ground on the more important issues in our relationship. I was too programmed to give into my husband's wishes. Oh yes, I had scraped his dinner into the garbage a couple of times and after I started working, I remember one night, we had both put in a hard day at our jobs, picked the girls up at the daycare and upon arriving home, David went into the living room and turned on the television. Working a full-time job and being a full-time wife and mother was difficult, too. I had tried to bring up the subject of sharing the home responsibilities several times, but was tuned out. This night I simply went into the living room and sat in front of the television with David and the girls. Finally he turned to me and asked, "Well, aren't we going to have dinner?"

"Yes," I replied, "as soon as you get into the kitchen and start peeling the potatoes, I will cook the meat." I was finally heard and we divided household chores in a way that was fair and that part of our family life began to run very smoothly.

Finally I came up with an idea that would give me the ability to help supplement the family income and stay at home. Depression got the best of me at one point because of having to leave my children and medication had been prescribed. When my Doctor advised that I could probably do without it, I had a very hard time. It was then that I realized, **problems must be solved and not postponed.** In my case, I felt the medication just pushed the problems into the background. I reasoned that every challenge had a solution and the best way to solve a problem was to approach it head-on and find the solution. Postponing it or pushing it into the background sometimes made it worse.

I proposed the idea to David and it appealed to him. We could buy a piano; I could go back to taking lessons, work towards a degree and teach students. The idea was launched. The only problem was that when my husband realized the financial potential, I was continually pressured to take on more and more students. The time for teaching had to be outside of school time, so after school and Saturdays were soon filled with students coming and going. I was home during the day and became very adept at organizing meals, cooking, cleaning, laundry, sewing and all the things that needed to be done to keep a household running smoothly. The yard work was in my job description as well. Three hours a day were devoted to my own piano practice and study of theory, harmony, history and counterpoint. How did I manage? I became very efficient at organizing my time and using every resource at my disposal.

We were finally on top financially and David even started being more involved as a parent. Because I took students Saturday mornings, that became an opportunity for him to spend quality time with our girls. Finally, when our youngest daughter was eight years old, David consented to having another child. Another daughter was born and we managing very well. It had taken many years and much work to get to this point. Most couples will tell you that the first 15 years of a marriage are the hardest.

I had a close friend whose experience was similar to mine but at the 15 year point things got worse instead of better. Her husband got romantically involved with a co-worker.

At first, she was unaware of the affair. She only sensed that there was something wrong in the relationship. After assessing what she could see from her perception she tried to talk to her husband, Glen, about it but she found him un-cooperative. So, in trying to find a solution herself, she reasoned that they just needed to spend more time together. She first reorganized her work schedule so there was more together time on weekends. This totally backfired on her as the only thing Glen could see was a reduction in income.

Glen came to my friend Kara at the end of January that year and told her he needed some time to go off by himself to work some things out. She was so anxious to resolve the problem that she even packed his bags for him and put love notes in shirt pockets, pant pockets and every little nook and cranny she could think of. She wouldn't let herself face reality, but of course that was the first time she had to deal with her husband having an affair, so what did she know? She found out the truth when the mother of Glen's mistress called the house to see if Kara knew how to get in touch with Glen and her daughter. Kara found out later that many people knew what was going on, but were reluctant to tell her. She could totally understand that because one is never sure what to do in situations like these.

When Kara finally heard from Glen, he called to say he was sorry; he had made a mistake. Could she forgive him? He would like to come home from New Zealand where he had followed his new love. Again, because of her inexperience she accepted him home. Glen assured Kara that he had learned his lesson and was home to stay. In reality he had just come back to file his income tax and make final arrangements to return to his girlfriend.

Glen left again and this time Kara finally faced the truth and began learning about the cruel realities of infidelity. She got in touch with a lawyer and was told she couldn't even file for divorce for seven years. Back then, this case was looked on as desertion and because Glen had gone to New Zealand, our Canadian system was unable to work through the legal system there.

After spending some time pitying herself she began to focus on her survival and that of her children. She was supported by caring friends and relatives who surrounded her, but it was Kara that had to figure out where she should go from there. Kara kept on working, took in sewing and managed to pay the bills. When summer came her hours at work were cut and the kids were off school so she took in more sewing to make up the shortfall. She would get up in the wee hours of the morning, it was hard to sleep anyway, and sew until her children got up. They would all have breakfast and plan their day. Kara's sister lived in a lake community nearby and so they planned to spend every nice afternoon swimming, picnicking and enjoying the summer with her at the lake.

One day in mid-July, the phone rang, and Kara recognized the voice on the other end. It was Glen. He was calling from the airport and wondered if Kara would come and pick him up. She was alone. Her sister had taken the children for a visit in another city for the day. All that Kara had been through over the past few months had taken its toll and she was emotionally numb. Hearing Glen's voice awakened no feelings in her. Kara agreed to go to the airport and when she saw her husband she was still without feeling. She couldn't feel anger toward him nor compassion or sympathy. He was thin and his face drawn. His once light brown hair mixed with grey had been dyed. Kara concluded it had been an attempt to make him look younger. It was evident that he was relieved when he saw the car. They placed his bags in the trunk and he got in the passenger side without a word. Silence prevailed on the drive to the home that had been theirs.

As soon as they came to a stop in the driveway, Glen climbed out of the car and immediately went to the big tree in the back yard. It had been taken from the yard of Kara's parents and transplanted into their own yard several years before. It had grown into a beautiful shade tree. Glen put his hands up and clung to one of the lower branches, hung his head and began sobbing. Kara simply went into the house and busied herself with household chores. She completely removed herself from his grief.

Finally Glen came into the house and asked if they could talk. He was invited to sit in a chair in the living room and Kara sat across the room from him. It was then that he began sharing his whole experience with her.

The affair began, as all affairs do, from a casual acquaintance and grew to a friendship, then intimacy and finally to plans for a life together. Blinded by excitement, desire and passion, plans were made to settle in New Zealand where they would be far away from anyone who knew them. There was no thought of how their decisions would affect family, friends or anyone to whom their lives were connected with in the past. The only problem was, when Glen returned to New Zealand after coming back to make his final arrangements, his girlfriend had found someone else and he was stuck! He was then forced into a rather solitary life, boarding with a family and simply working, saving money and finally making arrangements to make his way back home.

Glen said, "I know I have hurt you, and probably beyond any possibility for forgiveness. I just want to be near you and the children. If you want a divorce, you have it. I will work and help support you and our children all I can. I just want the opportunity to see the kids as much as you will let me." Then he handed her a big roll of money.

Kara was still feeling no emotion, but she took the money and told him that much time, thought and watching to see if his promises could be trusted would have to be the basis for any decisions made about them. Talk was cheap at this point. His children needed him to be in their lives, however, and he was welcome to visit only, but he would have to live elsewhere.

By then the children had arrived home from their visit. Kara's oldest daughter was, to say the least, reserved and sceptical. She was a teenager and had been more aware of the situation. The middle child welcomed his dad with open arms as did their youngest. Kara invited Glen to stay for dinner so he could be with the children and she just stayed in the background. After dinner a call was made to Glen's brother. He and his wife agreed to let him come and stay with them.

Glen visited every evening, got a job and gave Kara all he earned except for what he needed to pay for his board and room. After several months, their son said to Kara, "Don't you think you've made Dad suffer long enough?" The oldest daughter and Kara had a hard time trusting him, but after much consulting with her lawyer, who was also a family friend and considering what was best for her little family, she agreed to try again.

The life of a single mother is hard and Kara felt that alone she would not be able to provide for her children in a way that they deserved. Even though she knew that coming home to her was Glen's second choice, for if his girlfriend had not found someone else, he would still be in New Zealand. But if he would be good to them, be a support as a father and provider, Kara could be content, knowing that her children had what they needed.

So the rebuilding process began and Glen walked his talk. He worked hard, struggled with issues that resulted from his guilt, and actually became a much better father. Kara learned to trust him again and worked on her own forgiveness. Two years later they agreed to have another child and were blessed with another son.

What can be learned from this experience? Three important truths. The first one is that we usually contribute to our situation in one way or another. In not standing up for ourselves when pressured to take on more work in order to make more money or any other responsibility that pushes us beyond our ability to maintain a balance, we often cause our relationships to suffer. True, it takes both partners in a marriage to recognize the same truth, as relationships are two-sided and each partner needs to take equal responsibility putting in the same time and effort, but someone needs to take the lead and unfortunately sometimes neither partner is willing. It is often said, "No matter how thin you slice the cheese, there are two sides!" The second truth is that forgiveness is a process, not an event, and it is acceptable for a person to take time to work on forgiving. The third one is that family has to come first. When two people bring children into the world, their responsibility is to provide for the needs of those children.

Glen and Kara were married many more years before he passed away. There were several rocky places in the marriage and even though Kara always felt she was Glen's second choice, she knew she had made the best decision for their family in keeping the unit together.

Marriage is a lot of work for each partner. I was speaking to a man who was on his third marriage. When asked if he felt that he was happier in his present marriage and that his choice to divorce the other two times led him to his current happiness, his reply was, "If I had worked as hard at my first marriage as I am in my present one, I would still be married to my first wife."

Now we all know that there are many situations and circumstances that need individual consideration. If one is in an abusive partnership, and if the abusive partner is unwilling to get help, sometimes the decision to get out has to be made. However, we live in a throw-away society and often we give up, thinking that problems can be solved by walking away. In most cases, we carry our problems with us. When we take responsibility for our contribution to deteriorating situations, problems can be solved, marriages and relationships saved.

ACCEPTANCE OF DIFFERENCES:

The first big difference that needs to be accommodated is simply the difference between men and women in general. Many books have been written on this subject, with suggestions on how to accept and deal with them. Problems arise when we expect our partner to automatically respond to situations the same way we do and 'see it our way.' It is much more realistic to expect that they will have a different point of view and we must be open to understand the way they see it. When we are seeking to understand in any negotiation, we can learn that there are many ways of seeing things and doing things.

RESPECT:

Everyone has a right to be here, to occupy a space in the world and a chance to grow and learn. Everyone has the right to be loved, to set and maintain their own boundaries and to develop their own belief system based on their own experiences. Everyone has the right to make his or her own choices based on that belief system.

Recognizing that each individual has rights was the motivation behind the creation of a democratic government. Laws are established to ensure that individual rights are respected. Authority figures are put in place to ensure safety, the protection of rights and that everyone is treated fairly. I sometimes wonder if there would be more successful marriages if each couple had an authority figure that monitored their relationship ensuring the safety, protection of rights and fair treatment or each person involved.

The most successful partnership occurs when two strong people choose to share each others lives. A strong person is one who acknowledges and accepts his or her own value. They have learned to take care of themselves physically, emotionally, intellectually, socially and spiritually. They know that happiness is a result of what happens inside them instead of looking outside for validation.

Dysfunction occurs when the relationship gets out of balance because one partner wants or has a need to control, and one partner enables the other by giving up their rights. The enabler always gives in just so it will seem that the two of them are getting along. Both partners lose when this happens. The controlling partner, in getting their way all the time, is deprived of learning flexibility, sharing, acceptance of differences, understanding, compassion and opportunities to develop forgiveness. They are deprived of the opportunity to be in a place where they learn the value of opening themselves to the many sides and possible approaches and solutions to any issue.

The one who enables is unable to use their creativity where exploration and experimentation aids growth and learning. They give up their right to make choices and learn from the choices they make.

Every human being is gifted, talented and has much to offer and share. When both partners in a marriage feel free to contribute, when they know the other partner respects them, recognizes and values the others strengths, differences can be celebrated and the relationship enhanced.

COMMUNICATION:

Each experience in our human existence is accompanied by an emotion. Humans have a whole range of emotions, some negative and some positive. Many people find it easy to allow themselves to feel and have learned to process their feelings in ways that support them. They can easily find the words to talk about their feelings and communication comes natural.

It was discussed in chapter two that as little children often we learn that having positive feelings such as excitement, happiness, contentment, peace, joy and gratitude brings acceptance and positive attention. We learned that negative feelings such as anger, sadness, fear, guilt and disappointment bring rejection because often those feelings are expressed with negative behavior which brought negative attention. When the negative behavior was corrected, they may have gotten the message that the feeling was bad as well as the way they expressed it. Because children want positive attention, praise, rewards and acceptance they often learn to stuff their negative feelings. Behavior can then be checked, but it sometimes blocks the learning of communication skills, particularly the ability to put feelings into words. Sometimes children even get the message that when they have positive feelings they are 'good' and having negative feelings makes them 'bad'.

In reality, feeling emotions just makes us human. It

is normal and natural to have feelings. Positive feelings tell us all is well in our world. Negative feelings simply tell us there is something emotional that we need to take care of.

For example, it is natural to feel anger when we have seen or experienced an injustice. Anger is an emotion that should motivate us to make right a wrong. If we never felt fear, we would get ourselves into dangerous situations. Guilt and remorse help us to maintain our integrity. Sadness and disappointment help us to feel compassion. Feeling our feelings helps us to identify with the feelings of others.

Negative feelings are neither good nor bad. They are just feelings. They help to make us human and can be very useful. How we act on those feelings, however, can be judged as good or bad. If we act on our feelings in a way that shows disrespect, invades the other's boundaries without permission or harms others, the outcome of our decision to act on our feelings in this way is negative, or bad.

In our society, it has become more socially acceptable for females to express their feelings. In many cases males are taught to hide their emotions. This is one of the major factors that cause communication problems between couples. It is what keeps one partner from being able to relate to or understand how the other is feeling. Good communication begins with compassion. It is important to bring up an issue soon after a problem is evident, discuss it, resolve it and then never bring it up again. If a problem is buried and not addressed it will surface again and again, undermining the relationship.

WILLINGNESS TO FORGIVE:

A most unrealistic expectation in marriage is that we will never experience hurt. In any relationship there are occasions when disagreements and misunderstandings are going to occur. Whether we are hurt through unintentional or intentional means, our ability to forgive will often mean success in being able to move through the experience rather than getting stuck in it.

To forgive means to lose the desire for revenge. Forgiveness serves best the one who needs to forgive. Carrying the hurt encumbers growth because energy is focused on the problem instead of the solution.

REALISTIC EXPECTATIONS:

Realistic expectations protect couples from being blindsided when differences become evident. People grow and change as life goes on. Expecting differences and change allows us to be flexible and accepting when they occur. Flexibility and acceptance give us resiliency. Then, when what happens is different than we expected, we can deal with it in a positive way.

Dealing with the unexpected in a positive way is what gives us the ability to really live "happily ever after."

Throughout the child's life parents work toward preparing them to leave home.

CHAPTER SIX
OUR CHILDREN ARE NOT OURS

I have often thought that parenting would be so much easier if each of our children came with an instruction manual. For most of us, parenting skills are learned from our imperfect parents. Through the experiences and perceptions of our youth we begin to form opinions of parenting methods and many of us vow, "I will never raise my kids the way my parents raised me and my siblings." By the time the first child arrives, theories and ideas on how to do it the "right way" have been formed.

I used to think that raising children would be like following a recipe. You simply took one child, added lots of love and learning experiences, a little discipline, training and teaching, took care of all the physical needs such as feeding, keeping the nose wiped and the bottom dry and the result would be a happy well adjusted adult, who loved you and would be grateful for all your efforts. *Wrong!* What went missing in my recipe were all the unknowns that each child comes with. Each is a product of a unique mixture of genes from parents and grandparents as well as their own unique processing from their learning experiences.

With the decision to become a mother or father should also come a commitment to provide everything that child needs, not only physically, but emotionally, intellectually, socially and spiritually, because the child is completely dependent on us in the beginning. Throughout the child's life parents work toward preparing them to leave home. If a child fails to become independent it is usually regarded as a sign that mother and father have failed.

Parents are the teachers and children are the students. The parents' job is to teach and the child's job is to listen. Because eighty percent of communication is non-verbal, a child will learn more from what he observes than what has been taught through verbal communication. How many parents have experienced frustration when they tell and tell, but the second half of the teaching equation has failed to occur? Children learn best what they experience. It is true that actions speak louder than words.

Because children want to believe their family functions with patterns that are normal, they will defend their family pattern, even if it is dysfunctional. The media can help a child to identify dysfunction but it can also justify it. Only when the circle they are influenced by extends outside their own family, do they begin to realize that families can function different than their's.

Gradually, as skills for independence are taught, it is important to help each child form realistic self-expectations on their own. As a parent endeavors to ensure that their expectations of each child are realistic during the maturing process, most children learn that forming expectations is a valuable motivator. Unrealistic expectations placed on a child from the parent can be very damaging to self-esteem and to the parent/child relationship.

Every parent eventually learns that their children are not really theirs, that they don't own them. These precious visitors only pass through their influence for a time. Eventually the parents learn to let go and allow the relationship to change from caregiver to friend. Inter-relating on an adult-to-adult level can then be achieved and enjoyed.

Since parents are not required to take classes or pass a test before they have children, the only way for us to learn about parenting is through the experiences of others.

WORTH THE WAIT

Anne sat staring out of the window. "What have I done wrong?" she asked herself. For as long as she could remember, Anne had wanted to be a mother. How could something she looked forward to with so much joy end up bringing so much pain? She was a small woman in her late sixties. In spite of a lifetime of challenges and work, Anne had aged well, always mistaken for ten years younger. But the silver hair that framed her heart-shaped face always gave her away. She dressed in good taste with her hair styled to compliment the mature, yet youthful demeanor. The happy countenance that seemed to illuminate from her had attracted many life-long friends. Children had always been drawn to her, and she still loved to work with them.

"Why," she asked herself, "can I make friends with anyone I choose to, except my Elizabeth?" Elizabeth was Anne's oldest child. The baby daughter was so wanted, so loved and was the first to give Anne that joy only a mother can experience with the arrival of a new baby. This little person had represented the realization of her life-long dream. As Elizabeth approached middle age, she more and more resembled her mother. People had quit commenting on it in Elizabeth's presence because they could see her stiffen whenever it was brought up.

"What did I do wrong?" Anne asked herself again. She knew she had made mistakes as a mother. Children don't come with instruction manuals tied to their big toe. But Anne had done the best she could. The first clue that their relationship was in trouble, came at the birth of Anne's first grandchild, when Elizabeth's husband had called to announce the big event. Anne had answered the phone in the wee hours of the morning.

"It's a boy," he had said, with pride in his voice.
"How is Elizabeth?" Anne had queried.

"She did just great and is fine," he replied.

"We can hardly wait to see him. When can we come?" Ann was anxious. "Would right now be O.K.?" She knew it was a silly question; it was the middle of the night after all. But she was so anxious to see and hold her first grand child.

"No." The voice was firm. "It may be a day or two. We'll let you know when we are ready".

Anne could still feel the disappointment and confusion. Anne had expected that her daughter would be anxious for a visit from the new grandparents.

As time went on it became very evident that Elizabeth resented many things about her parents. "I only want you to talk to Matt when I'm around to hear you," she had said one day. "I will need to monitor what you say to him."

Anne was shocked. She loved children and related to them so well. Why would her daughter feel she needed to protect her son from his grandparents?

Being a very spiritual person, Anne had prayed often for answers and guidance to help her resolve the differences between her and her daughter. She seemed to get answers to all her other prayers, why not his one? Anne tried to talk it out, but Elizabeth was silent. Through it all, as more children were born, Anne was hopeful that one day, she would be able to get it right.

There was one Christmas, just after the birth of another baby; Anne had visited to see how things were going. Elizabeth was distraught because the decorations on the tree were gradually getting destroyed by the toddler as the newborn was nursing. Anne devised a plan. After Christmas, she would get an artificial tree and during the year, hand-make child-proof ornaments. This gift would be just the colors Elizabeth would want. At one of the family gatherings through the holidays that year, Anne found an opportunity to casually inquire of Elizabeth about her likes and dislikes in Christmas decorations. "Elizabeth, do you and George prefer real trees at Christmas or do you think artificial ones are nice?"

"I think artificial ones are O.K.," Elizabeth answered. "Why do you ask?"

Anne pondered over her next thought. "I was just wondering. A lot of people are getting the artificial ones because they are safer."

"Yes, that is certainly something to consider," came the answer, with a suspicious look.

"Which do you like better," Anne went on, "decorations in traditional Christmas colors, or ones that match the decor in the room?"

"What are you trying to say, Mom?" Elizabeth had snapped. "Now you don't like the way our Christmas tree looks?"

"No, I was just wondering," Anne said trying to hide her hurt.

"Matching the decor, I guess," Elizabeth had finally replied. All their conversations seemed to end in misunderstanding.

Determined, Anne went ahead with her plan. An artificial tree was purchased at an after Christmas sale and throughout the year every spare minute was spent crocheting, knitting, working plastic canvas, sewing and stuffing until by the next Christmas she had a whole Christmas tree full of ornaments that could be thrown, chewed, pulled, yanked, sat or stomped on, and they would survive.

When the gift was presented three weeks before the next Christmas, for the first time in the many years of a strained relationship, Elizabeth expressed gratitude. Tears welled up as she said, "What a thoughtful gift."

The 'warming up' was short-lived though, and everything returned to the way it had been before. One of the aspects of this problem that hurt Anne the most was how it had affected her relationship with her grandchildren. They seemed like strangers to her. The oldest grandson had experienced many problems as he grew up. Anne wished she could help, but held back for fear of retribution.

Her husband had always said, "You're going to have to stop fretting about this.

You will be able to form a relationship with those kids, only when they grow up and are away from their mother."

When Matt turned twenty-two, Anne and her husband invited him over for dinner. Soon it became a weekly event that everyone looked forward to. A very special relationship developed. Then when the oldest granddaughter, Amy, got married, three dinner guests were at the table.

Now, as Anne sat looking out the window warm feelings came over her as she reflected on the cherished moments she had shared with her adult grandchildren. She startled, as the ring of the phone interrupted her thoughts. Picking up the phone, she heard the voice on the other end of the line. It was familiar, but the tone was unexpectedly warm.

"Mom?"

"Yes," Anne replied.

"I need to share something with you." It was Elizabeth.

It was the first of many conversations and experiences that began to draw the two of them together. Elizabeth never shared the reason for the long separation with her mother and Anne never pried. It was enough that her prayer had been answered; she just had to wait awhile.

MY OWN WAY

Carolyn could sense the wall between her and Karen building all through the summer. The little girl that had been the kind, gentle peacemaker in the family had now grown into a woman and during her last year at college had met a young man. The more Carolyn and Dean found out about the young man, the more concerned they became. Karen had indicated that she and Jim were talking about getting married and yet there was no effort on Jim's part to drive the ten hours to visit Karen or meet her family during the three months they were separated. There had been many conversations with their daughter, where Carolyn and Dean had tried to point out the danger signs that they saw developing in the relationship, but Karen only became more withdrawn and defensive.

Karen had returned to school and she became more separated from her family in ways other than just the miles between them. Carolyn and Dean became so worried at one point that they phoned Karen's school counselor to ensure that their daughter was all right.

Christmas break came and Karen came home to celebrate with her family. Then she rushed back to spend New Year's Eve with Jim and his family. A few months later a phone call came.

"Hello, this is Jim." The voice was cold. "Karen and I are getting married in March. You can come if you want to, but it really doesn't matter whether you do or not, we are getting married anyway."

"Well of course we want to be there," Carolyn had replied. "But can't we help plan the wedding? We could have it here; we would like to help out."

"No, we are going to keep it simple. We will be married at my parents' home and then just go out for Chinese food after. Come if you want to."

Her daughter's wedding day arrived. "You've got to quit crying," Carolyn said to herself. "You know how your nose turns red when you cry. Get a hold of yourself. You want to appear happy for Karen on her special day."

Earlier that morning Carolyn had written down her feelings on the motel stationery. Writing had always been a good way to get her feelings out when it wasn't the right time to express them to the person with whom she really needed to communicate. She wrote:

Dear Karen and Jim,

I'm writing this because right now Dean and I feel we won't be given a chance to say it in person and we feel it needs to be said. It is important to us that you are given the opportunity to understand how we feel at this time.

We know you must love each other very much right now. We hope that you may learn to love each other more as the years pass. We are just sorry our relationship with you as a couple, started out this way. I guess this is an example of the problems that come when people stop communicating. We understand how you feel, but sense that you do not accept that we are even trying to understand.

I'm sure you sensed that we were trying to pressure you into waiting or getting married another way and I suppose we were, in a way. You must know however, that it was out of love for you and a concern for your future together. We have learned through experience that it is easier to prevent causing hurt rather than trying to patch things up once the damage has been done. We have also learned that others forgive you more readily and you can forgive yourself once you recognize that you have done something to hurt another. This always means that one must attempt to see things from another's point of view.

We recognize that you have felt hurt because it has been difficult for us to accept the decisions you have made and things were said over the phone on both sides that caused hurt feelings. I know that because we are older, we are also supposed to be wiser. The reality is no matter how old we get, when we get hurt, the tendency is to lash out and hurt back. Dean and I are still struggling with our immaturity in this area, so I hope you will forgive us for this weakness.

Being a parent brings with it many responsibilities

and as we fulfill these, we feel it earns us certain rights and privileges. Bringing Karen into the world brought with it a responsibility to teach her and encourage all the growth and learning possible in order for her to realize her potential. We taught her that each person has a purpose in life and a mission. In order to help her fill this we had to learn as much as we could along the way and then impart this knowledge to her. Along with this came the responsibility of caring for her physical needs - food, clothing, and a warm comfortable home. But we didn't mind the work, it was a privilege. I tease her about her having colic and keeping me up all night when she was little. It got so bad at one point that she got her nights and days mixed up.

In spite of all the work, I loved being her mother. She was always so happy, even when she had the mumps, if you can believe it! She would never give in to sickness, but had a great way of "pretending herself well" again. Wrapping her dad and me around her little finger was one of her greatest talents and although it usually got her what she wanted, she was also always the first to forgive.

I could write a book on her attributes, but I'm sure it is because of these that you love her, Jim, so I won't list them. I only want you to know that we know how special she is and because we know it, with all our faults and failings and with our small capacity for love compared to Heavenly Father, imagine how special she is to Him.

Another one of our responsibilities was to train her to be self-sufficient because one day, we knew she would leave us. Although we knew we would miss her, we hoped she would choose a mate that would cherish her as we did and would help her to progress even more than she had with us.

We don't know you very well, Jim. That is probably why it is hard for us to accept the way you and Karen decided to get married. Your phone call telling us that it was going to happen with or without our presence, that we could be there if we wanted to, but our participation was not important to either of you, was very hurtful.

In another phone conversation you said that close family relationships were important and yet your actions thus far have told us otherwise. Perhaps as we get to know you better, we will also understand you better. Time will tell.

I guess, since a wedding is the last thing a father does for his daughter, understandably he wants it to be very special. The daughter's desires are very important, but what ever they were, we would have liked to been given the opportunity to contribute and make the wedding as nice as we could. We felt robbed of this privilege. We have nothing against you personally; we just want the very best for Karen, because we love her so much. I pray that both of you will forgive us for any hurt we have caused you. We wish you both a happy life together. Our daughter's happiness lies now in the life you create together and we promise to support you the best we can in the decisions you make.

All our love,

Mom and Dad

Carolyn had gone to her daughter's wedding and the dinner at the restaurant that followed. She tried her best to hide the disappointment she felt and the anxiety over her daughter's future. Karen seemed happy and that was enough for now. Being sensitive to the circumstances at the time, Carolyn decided to wait for an opportunity in the future to give the letter to Karen, so it was tucked away in the luggage and carried the 700 miles home.

During the next few years, Carolyn and Dean visited as often as time and distance would permit, always trying to be positive and supportive as they observed Karen's situation.

When Karen informed her parents after giving birth, that they had a beautiful granddaughter, they excitedly drove to the town where their daughter was living and knocked on the apartment door. When Jim opened it he said, "Oh, it's you," and then closed the door again, leaving Carolyn and Dean on the landing. Stunned at first, they then looked at each other and began discussing which motel they should book into when Karen re-opened the door. They were invited in. Apprehensively, to say the least, the invitation was accepted and the rest of the visit seemed to go well.

Carolyn and Dean learned many years later that there had been a misunderstanding that had caused the incident but at the time it was very hurtful. Even though they were hurt, a determined effort was made to maintain a relationship with their daughter, her husband and now their granddaughter.

Eventually another little girl came along. Karen warmly welcomed her parents each time they made the trip, but Jim was always cool. He displayed signs of heavy drinking and each time they visited things were worse than the time before. Carolyn and Dean were always worried that their daughter covered up her situation so that they wouldn't suspect the worst.

Karen began making trips home to visit, driving herself and her two daughters. They planned vacations at a lake in the summer on two occasions and Karen brought her two daughters up so they could all be together. There were other occasions when Carolyn and Dean met their daughter halfway on the long trip between cities, picked up their granddaughters and took them to their home for a visit. They would then return with the same travel arrangements. There were two occasions when Jim agreed to come when Karen's younger siblings were married, but most of the time it was just Karen and her girls. It was always worth the effort as a strong bond developed between Carolyn, Dean, Karen and the two beautiful girls as they were growing up.

Fifteen years went by and finally one night Carolyn and Dean were awakened by the phone ringing.

"Mom?" said the voice at the other end of the line. Carolyn recognized Karen's voice.

"Can I come home?" she tearfully said. "Can I bring the girls? Can we live with you until I can get established?"

"Of course you can," relied Carolyn. This will always be your home. What has happened?"

Dean got on another phone and they both heard their daughter tell about the events over the past fifteen years. She had endured years of living with an abusive alcoholic which had led to her decision to call. Karen then assured her parents, "The girls and I are safe and I booked us into a motel. I will call again tomorrow and we can talk about arrangements." The conversation ended but Carolyn and Donna's worst fears had been realized.

Donna got out a letter she had received from her daughter many years before. As she re-read it, she compared the hurt and fear she had sensed in her daughter's voice with some of the lines her daughter had written when she was so sure of herself. She had written:

Dear Mom and Dad;

Now that I have my head on straight and I've had time to think clearly about what you said, I've talked it out with Jim and I'm not going to say what I think you want to hear. First, I want you to know that my mind is made up. I am going to marry Jim, mostly because I love him, but also for the person he is and what he believes.

I guess the biggest thing parents must learn from their children is that everyone has to lead their own lives. Remember "Fiddler on the Roof?" One of the daughters chose to go her own way and live their own life and the father never accepted it. After that, she never saw her family or associated with them. I can easily foresee that happening in our family and it really disturbs me. It's a big decision I've made and in my mind I've made the best decision for me.

I'm not making it because I think I'll be unhappy, nor have I jumped into it lightly thinking everything will be a bed of roses. I think you must have known I was deciding this summer, when I was home from college. Just like everyone else, we will have problems, but I know us and our relationship. I know we will be very, very, happy.

If you're thinking, "Where did we go wrong?" Well I'll tell you right now, you didn't go wrong. When we learn, we each learn from our own perspective, and that is what makes us individuals. I retained different things that you did and that is why I think the way I do. One thing I have learned is that you can't be happy trying to live your life the way someone else wants you to and so I've decided to make myself happy with my life instead of pleasing everyone else. I'm writing this letter very carefully, hoping that you can fully understand how I'm feeling. I think once you know why I have decided what I have it will ease the tension between us. So, I am going to say it again, I am going to marry Jim!

Jim and I want to have a good relationship with you. We are both concerned about that, so please understand. I love you very much and I know that Jim will too, once he gets to know you better, because that's the way you are. Please let me be your daughter.

Love Karen

Carolyn then read the letter she had written in the motel room fifteen years earlier. She had always meant to share it with Karen, but through the years there never seemed to be an appropriate time. One lesson that had been learned over those years is that parents can't make decisions for their children and they can't save them from experiencing the outcome of those decisions. Sometimes parents are unable to agree with the decisions their children make but what they need to respect is their children's right to make them. One of the hardest things that parents learn to do is give love to their children even though what they do sometimes seem undeserving of love and respect.

Karen was unable to return to her home with Carolyn and Dean as her children were born in one country and her parents lived in another. She was afraid of a legal battle over the children if she tried to take them out of the country. As time went on, Karen and Jim did get divorced. Carolyn and Dean assisted some, but they had indeed helped their daughter to learn self-reliance and she bounced back. Karen had a good job and was able to work her way up in her chosen profession until she was very self-sufficient financially. She eventually married again to a man who she thought really cherished and loved her.

The relationship between Karen and her parents grew stronger and stronger as Carolyn and Dean made visits to her a priority. Then Karen got the news that her dad was dying. She and her new husband traveled home to visit her parents several times and when her father passed away, of course, they were there for Carolyn.

Karen was very attentive to her widowed mother.

There was not a week that went by that she didn't call her and there were many visits made back and forth. The mother/daughter relationship developed into a very strong bond. It was a relationship which evolved on an adult-to-adult level that they both valued and enjoyed with mutual respect on both sides.

A few years went by and when Carolyn decided to get married again, Karen was a very enthusiastic supporter. She knew what it was like to be alone and wanted her mother to have the secure companionship that marriage can bring.

Karen worked so hard to make her own marriage work. She struggled with trying to get her new husband's children to accept her. Even though they were all adults, each had their own agenda and seemed determined to divide Karen and her husband.

Her own girls were unhappy as well and it was difficult for Karen to make decisions that were acceptable to her new husband. She was often torn between what she felt was right, supporting her own children and making choices that simply kept the peace. After a valiant effort, she finally had to come to the realization that this marriage had also failed. Karen asked her mother one day, "Why is this always happening to me?"

Carolyn tried to answer but felt her daughter shutting down. She guessed it was because after all this time, Carolyn was saying things Karen didn't want to hear. Her daughter was determined to make "her way" work for her. In many ways it had, but Karen had always been the kind of person who seemed to be blind to the red flags in relationships. Because she was so kind it was hard for her to accept that others could be unkind, manipulative and controlling. Often she gave others the benefit of the doubt to the point that she put herself in situations that were unhealthy for her. Each person will learn their life's lessons in their own time and way. Sometimes they must repeat a mistake several times before they learn from it. All parents can do is encourage their offspring to take responsibility for their choices, learn from their mistakes and get up again every time they fall down.

Happiness is all that any parent wants for their child. They just hope that doing things *their way* will bring them the life they want.

THE INTRUDER

When Emma was born, Laura was taking piano lessons. In fact everyone wondered if the baby would be born with a piano between its toes. When it was confirmed that she was pregnant, Laura was working on a certain Hayden Sonata, and ever after she was no longer pregnant she would feel nauseous when she heard it, because she was working on the piece in the first few weeks of pregnancy when morning sickness was part of the daily ritual.

Emma was very special to her mother, partly because she had begged her husband to consent to another baby for a very long time before he finally gave in. But she was a naturally loving child and filled the longing when maternal instincts, ones only a woman can identify with, kicked in. As she got older the relationship between Emma and Laura blossomed even more. Sure Emma had a few rebellious years, as every teenager does, but it was when Laura experienced her severe depression that they really became close. The mother/daughter talks became Laura's life line. Emma had pulled her through the darkest days of her life.

One great attribute Emma possessed was her ability to speak her mind. She had learned to stand up for herself very effectively mostly because she and her father had personalities so much alike. They reacted to everything in a similar way, so when there was a confrontation between them they bounced off each other. Sometimes it got so bad that Laura had to intervene and referee, but Emma had certainly learned to speak her mind. Laura often said, "You don't need to wonder what Emma is thinking because she always tells you." Perhaps that was another reason why the mother/daughter relationship was so strong when Emma got married. The two of them always spoke their minds and were able to resolve differences as they came along, instead of allowing them to fester.

Emma's choice for a lifetime partner was a very kind, sensitive, loving man. Laura and her husband respected and adored him right from the start. In fact, when Emma asked her mother on one occasion, "If Tony and I ever had an argument, you would probably take his side, wouldn't you mom?"

"Probably," was the reply.

When the wedding was being planned, Emma asked her mother to do something for the program at the reception. Laura knew that if she tried to do something serious she would just cry so she decided to write a humorous reading for the occasion.

A GIRL AND HER BATHROOM

In the duplex on the city drive and right on
    up the stairs,
The little room set waiting, the family had
    prepared.
All laid out in grand display and neatly in a
    row,
Were all the things a baby needs to keep
    clean as it grows.
This little room, it must be shared with one
    more family member,
The news spread quickly 'round about,
    'twas of the female gender.

Now Dad liked clean and tidy rooms, a neat
    freak pure and simple,
But loved this little baby girl who sported
    two sweet dimples.
So he'd put up with baby soap, powder, oil
    and rattles,
He knew out numbered four to one, t'would
    be a losing battle.
It wouldn't be forever, she would grow up
    some day,
Patiently he would wait 'til then, and then
    he'd have his way.

So day-by-day 'mid the array of Q-Tips,
    pins and lotions,
He sifted out his shaving gear and all his
    other notions.

*Soon toys were needed in the tub to keep
  up to Emma's demands,
One entering that bathroom now was taking
  his life in his hands.*

*The powder, oil, Q-Tips and lotions were re-
  placed by band-aids and bows,
Curlers, hair pins and all things used by little girls, everyone knows.
And each day all icky and gritty, dad put up
  with sand on the floor,
Now with a little boy baby, dear old dad
  was pushed out the door.*

*This problem it now needed solving, the so-
  lution was really quite near,
A new house containing two bathrooms was
  needed it was very clear.
So pack up and move did the family and
  dad thought to heaven he'd went,
A room of his own to keep tidy, to live like
  this he was just meant.*

*Meanwhile the other big bathroom was fill-
  ing with girl things galore,
Like soap, shampoo, dryers, steam rollers,
  with hair spray, toothpaste and more.
Our Emma she is into playing with Barbie
  and Ken dolls it seems,
Dad's cleaning the sink trap so often; he's
  doing it now in his dreams.
There's tiny shoes, earrings, belts, neck-*

laces, all stuck in the drain pipes below,
Dear dad a true hero can fix it, his gray
hair's beginning to show.

Now Emma's beginning to notice that more
fun than dolls are the boys.
And ten new kinds of shampoo line the tub
instead of toys.
A nail brush, loofa brush, face soap, lady
shaver and what else, who knows,
On the vanity lined up in all hues, is the pol-
ish for nails and toes,

Blush, eye liner, creams and mascara, curl-
ing irons, steam rollers, much more,
Pick, necklace, combs, ribbons, elastics
and mirrors just to add to the store.
In alcohol earrings are soaking, new con-
tact solutions array,
The top of vanity's gone now, the sink it just
faded away.

Poor dad he is fit to be tied now, with
Emma's new hair style she needs,
Mousse. And dad is just thinking, a moose
in the bathroom to feed?
A moose in the bathroom, now really, we're
carrying this ever too far.
No room just to mention the clean up - and
how will it fit in the car?
And how could a moose help our Emma to
fancy and fix her up fair?

The mousse my dear Dad is in a bottle, it's a
*   spray that you put in your hair.*

The other day Emma's intended, a big box
*   he packed and he took,*
Hauled it over to their apartment and Dad
*   snuck in the bathroom to look.*
The tub is all clean and all tidy, the vanity
*   really is there.*
The bathroom after all this time is none the
*   worse for wear.*

Dear boy we wanted to tell you, but felt we
*   should patiently wait,*
Until after you two were married and to back
*   out it would be late,*
We know you're a very fine fellow, and trust
*   that you'll overlook yet,*
The fact that the girl and her bathroom obvi-
*   ously come as a set.*

The wedding was a wonderful event and Laura cherished the relationship she had with both her daughter and new son-in-law. There were many family gatherings where love and respect were fostered and as children came along they only enhanced the relationships.

When Emma's father passed away after a brief illness, she and her husband were right there to support and comfort Laura. This continued all through the grieving process and Laura came to rely on their support.

Then, after a few years, Laura announced that she was going to remarry. Emma had a melt down, "How can you do this Mom? I don't know this man. How do you know he won't just take advantage of you? You don't expect me to accept him as my father do you? How much do you really know about him? You told me you were never getting married again. Do you know how complicated this is going to be? Aren't we enough to fill your life? How much more do you need?"

Finally there was a pause and Laura answered, "You kids have all been great. I couldn't have asked for more from you. But let's do the math. With dinner invitations from each of you, a couple of weeks, two times a year away at your sister's house, Easter, Christmas, Mother's Day and birthdays, I have about sixty days out of the year I can count on special times with my family."

"We have really tried hard to include you in our plans," Emma interrupted.

"I know and I'm not complaining. I don't expect you kids to make a life for me. On the other hand, I have three hundred days that I need to fill with projects, friends, experiences and everything that goes into making a life on my own. Then at the end of each day, except for when I visit your sister, I come home to an empty house and I go to bed alone," Laura reasoned.

"So what you're saying is that you're lonely?" asked Emma.

There was a pause, as Laura thought about her answer, "My life is full, and I can't say I am lonely, but I am alone. Could I bring Brian out to visit with you, Tony and the kids, so you can all meet him?"

"I will interrogate him, you have to know," Emma warned.

"That's okay," Laura said. "You have a right to ask anything you feel you need to."

The meeting went better that Laura expected. Brian handled all Emma's questions with confidence and Laura could sense that Emma was becoming less defensive. As time passed, communication between mother and daughter revealed why Emma had been so concerned. Life experiences had taught her that many women, in her mother's situation, are taken advantage of. Emma had always been her mother's protector and she was just trying to protect Laura now.

Once Emma got to know Brian better and began to trust that he was a person of integrity she began to accept the person who intruded on their relationship.

FOUR PLUS ONE CAN EQUAL TEN

"It's a boy," the doctor announced and Jessica felt the total joy that naturally comes with the birth of a new baby, but this time it was even more deeply felt because this child was an answer to much prayer.

Jessica and Ron had enjoyed the three girls who had been born to them but with every one, even though Ron had tried to hide it, the twang of disappointment at not having a son was sensed. All through the pregnancy Jessica had prayed that this time it would be a son. They had both agreed that they wanted to wait until the birth of the baby to know whether it was a boy or a girl. The time had finally arrived and Jessica thought, "I have enjoyed the girls, this child will be Ron's."

Jessica would come to discover that girls need

both a mother and father and so do boys. Parenting is definitely a team effort. Girls need a mother to provide the pattern of femininity and they need a father to help them learn how to relate to the opposite sex. Boys learn masculinity from their fathers and all about women from their mothers.

A very special bond developed between Jessica and her son, Brad, so much so that when he was grown and began dating, she began to fear that when he married that their relationship would have to change in a dramatic way. Jessica had noticed that for the most part, when sons married they seemed to attach themselves to their wife's family. "If that is the way it has to be, I will have to learn to live with it," she often thought. This mother had vowed that she would allow her children to make their own choices and go their own way. She felt strongly that the best gift someone can give their children is their freedom.

When Carol and Brad started getting serious, there was immediate acceptance on the part of the parents. Carol was bright, ambitious, and loving, and they loved having her in their home. Carol and Jessica would engage in long conversations about life and share opinions and ideas.

Finally, Jessica began to realize that she would never have to give up the relationship with her son; she had simply gained another daughter. She remembered her grandmother, who had four girls saying that it didn't matter whether you had boys or girls, that when they get married you often end up with an equal number of both in your family, anyway.

After Carol and Brad were married, it wasn't long

before a little granddaughter was added to the family. Carol's parents were wonderful people and she had a sister and brother in-law who had two boys.
Four plus one _CAN_ equal ten!

THE PREPARATION

She felt his tiny body,
Warm in her arms, their first son.
As she folded back the soft blanket
And examined the tiny toes and fingers,
She placed her finger in his little fist
And they watched as the tiny fingers closed
*   around it - for the first time.*

She steadied him,
Then allowing him his independence, let go.
As she watched him tottering toward his daddy,
He struggled to regain his balance,
She fought back the urge to steady him again,
And the little feet took steps on their own
*   - for the first time.*

They knelt beside him,
Night after night teaching him to give thanks
*   for all Divine gifts.*
"You are His child, He is mindful of you,"
*   They reassured.*
Faith grew, and he was able to find
*   His own words*
To express his feelings to his Heavenly
*   Father - for the first time.*

She laid out his new clothes.
He was full of excitement as he dressed himself.
They walked the distance together and his
little hand held hers, For reassurance.
Letting go, he walked away and then
Turned to wave good-bye.
With a lump in her throat, She watched him
As he went through the schoolhouse door
- for the first time.

They watched him struggle,
To read and understand the words
printed on the page.
She consoled him when he wondered
why he couldn't
Spend time playing like the other children.
Obediently he persisted with his daily program.
Finally, overcoming his handicap, he enjoyed a
victor's reward - for the first time.
She arranged all the pictures,
That would remind him of the ideas
he wanted to present.
He listened as his son practiced his presentation
over and over.
They watched him move to the microphone,
And then fight to control the fright of seeing
all those people,
He then heard his own voice over the loud speaker
- for the first time.

They looked on as he clutched the flag,
In his boyish hand and recited the Cub promise.

EXPECTATIONS

Each challenge prepared him for the next.
Striving to follow the Scouts promise,
He grew in spirit as he did physically.
Earning his Chief Scout award only inspired him
*   to earn his Queen Venture,*
And he became the one to receive that award
*   in his group - for the first time.*

He watched his father struggle,
To keep working when the pain was severe.
Selflessly he shouldered responsibilities
*   usually required only of adults,*
Health was regained and he witnessed
*   the miracle*
That only comes when prayers are answered.
Maturing in his ability to make decisions that
*   supported him*
He felt the capability and strength needed
*   for independence - for the first time.*

The announcement came,
"I want to be a Life Guard and teach swimming."
Taking the training, he then persevered when tests
*   needed*
To be re-done in order to qualify.
With confidence and courage he faced
*   the challenge of the job interview.*
Now, knowing he would be financially prepared
*   for his further education*
He felt secure in being able to reach his goal
*   - for the first time.*

"I am starting to have special feelings for Carol."
He told his mother.
"How do you know that this is the one?"
The feelings became stronger and stronger,
And soon there was talk of marriage
- for the first time.

They read it again,
The invitation to the event that would
bind two hearts as one.
With confidence he took the important step,
That he and his chosen one wanted and
Would ensure a happy future for both of them.
He smiled at his parents with gratitude
for their faith in him.
Watching through tear filled eyes,
they saw them walk away,
His hand was now in hers
for now it was their time.

SUMMARY

Successful family relationships can only develop when parents give their children freedom. Freedom to be who they are by celebrating the uniqueness in each child. Freedom to set their own expectations of themselves and the freedom to choose their own path.

When children are given freedom by their parents and they let go of expectations that interfere with their offspring's desire to choose their own path, a mutual respect is fostered between parents and children. It is realized that parents also have the freedom to make their own choices when children are mature enough to make theirs. The development of a relationship with one's adult children comes easier and can function on an adult-to-adult level. Realistic expectations on both sides become the foundation of the relationship.

All relationships begin, change, develop and will eventually close at some time.

CHAPTER SEVEN
CREATING CLOSURE

It was May 2000, and my husband announced he was going to retire. He had actually retired four times before but then found a job he could work at "just a little longer." In June, he resigned and assured me it was for the last time. In July, he started experiencing shortness of breath. In August, he was challenged with pain. That was when we decided he had better see a doctor.

During September, October and November we were referred to one specialist after another. Tests were taken and re-taken. We were always assured,

"We don't know what it is, but we know what it isn't. It isn't cancer." Finally, just before Christmas, after an ultra-sound had revealed a large mass around the left lung, my husband was admitted for surgery. It was decided that a biopsy was needed. After that surgery he was released just before the holidays, and we spent Christmas together and with our family.

January 6, 2001, the telephone rang. The surgeon said we could come to his office or he would talk to both of us over the phone. Being anxious to hear the results of the biopsy, we each got to a telephone and we both heard, "The results of the biopsy show you have a very rare, very aggressive form of cancer called Mesothelioma. It is untreatable. You have an appointment with the Tom Baker Cancer Centre in a few days. They will explain everything to you."

At the cancer clinic, we were given options, but essentially it was repetition of what we already knew. When I asked how long we had, we were told six months to four years. My husband died at home on February 28, 2001, less than two months after we found out.

Having lost my mother when I was 12 years old, and many relatives and friends after that, I was well acquainted with death. My dear grandmother, who had become my second mother, died 36 years after my mother had passed away and a short time later I lost my father. None of these impacted me as much as the loss of my husband. We had been married for 47 years.

During the time between diagnosis and death, we had prepared the best we could. But when the end came, I was hit with many things for which I was unprepared. All the while I was dealing with the unexpected, I had one thought, "I wish I could share what I have learned with others. Perhaps they would profit from my experiences and be better prepared to face what comes when their companion is taken, leaving them to deal with life alone".

I was overwhelmed with all the financial business and other details that had to be taken care of. I regretted having left so much of it up to my husband, thinking, "I will take care of the house and the major responsibility of raising the children. The finances, home maintenance and car are his responsibility." It is interesting how hindsight is so clear.

I had to learn about making a claim on insurance policies, how to manage investments and mutual funds. I had to acquaint myself with how our Registered Retirement Savings Plans (RRSPs) were set up as well as pension benefits.

Having a good knowledge of our bank accounts, both savings and checking, was an asset and I knew how to make deposits and withdrawals. But, I am embarrassed to say, I had never used a bank machine. I wasn't clear how our line of credit worked. I knew the house payments came out of our account each month with an automatic withdrawal, but had no idea how to arrange for that to happen. I had to learn about land titles and car financing.

I had always taken care of purchasing our groceries and clothing, but now there were utility bills (gas, lights, water and sewer), as well as telephone and property taxes. In addition there were insurance policies on the car, house and health that I had to be aware of and renew when they came due.

Income tax was in a category of its own. I learned the importance of keeping records and forms in order. Knowledge of tax exemptions is essential. If you don't claim all of them, the tax department is not going to inform you of those you missed.

I was grateful that I was well acquainted with our accountant. He was definitely a help and comfort. Our lawyer was certainly an asset and, in my view, essential. Other essentials are a Last Will and Testament and a Living Will. There is no question about inheritance with a Last Will and Testament. If the person who is ill is unable to communicate his or her desires regarding treatment or resuscitation, the Living Will gives instructions for caregivers which legally must be honored.

I gained knowledge about all government programs and pensions, including how to apply for benefits and what portion of the deceased spouse's benefits I was entitled to. Filling out government forms can be tedious, but it is the only way through the red tape.

I had to gain skills in home maintenance. Heating (taking care of the furnace); water (main valve in the house), winterizing the outside taps, how to fill the tank on the toilet so you can flush it even if the water gets turned off; lights (main panel, circuit breakers, re-set clocks); gas, what to do if the gas gets shut off (re-light pilot lights on the fireplace and hot water heaters, unless they have electrical starts). I also learned where to find the emergency numbers for all services. I had gained previous knowledge and skills with some of these items but had to learn others. It may seem trivial, but I even had to learn how to program the VCR - my husband had always controlled the control.

Car maintenance was my biggest challenge. I learned about spring and fall maintenance and the importance of having the belts and hoses checked. I needed knowledge about rotating tires, how to check tire pressure and change a tire. I became responsible for oil changes, filling the windshield washer fluid, checking the oil and filling the gas tank.

I was, however, prepared both emotionally and spiritually for this event in my life. I have a deep faith in the purpose of life and am able to draw support from divine sources. I just wish I had been more willing to learn, ahead of time, about all the physical and financial details I needed to know. I would have felt more secure, and could have moved through this difficult time easier. Knowledge is power. I knew some day I might have to experience the death of my spouse. I know that all relationships begin, develop and change. Every relationship we develop in life will at some time come to a close as well, either by choice or circumstance. Sometimes that circumstance is death. Death is an unavoidable part of life, but just knowing isn't enough.

My immediate concerns, of course, were the funeral arrangements and burial. Funeral homes are very efficient, and I was well cared for. However, prices for funerals can vary a lot in cost. A visit to several places to get information and price lists, well before a person is faced with the challenge, can be very enlightening. Also discussing wishes and preferences with your loved one ahead of time will make all the arrangements more meaningful. This is very hard for some and so it is put off. Sometimes there is time to do this even when a crisis occurs, but most often a death is sudden and no one is prepared.

Family and friends were such a support. Many people called to express their condolences. It was very comforting but at the same time stressful. I would hang up from one call and the phone would ring again, sometimes non-stop. It would have been so helpful for someone to be there to take calls, then pass the messages on to me. Answering machines can be so impersonal, especially at such an emotional time.

I live in a big city. I learned that it is wise to have someone stay in your home while everyone is at the funeral service. Funeral arrangements are announced in the newspaper, and there are those who may take advantage of an empty house. Sometimes a security system will take care of this concern.

After my husband's death, our bank's policy was to freeze all joint bank accounts in the event of a death. It was a protection, but also an inconvenience. Automatic withdrawals were honored, but no others. If I had been aware of this ahead of time, I would have had a bank account in my own name, with money available to take care of my immediate needs. There would have been lots of time to make arrangements for transferring the funds from the joint account to my new personal account and for the automatic withdrawals to come out of that one. Each bank has its own policy in this regard and it can differ from province to province. Being aware of each bank's policy in this matter can help a person to be prepared.

I had to change all utility accounts to be in only my name as well as property taxes. All Land Titles of jointly owned property, investments, RRSPs and car registrations needed to be in only my name as well.

Many documents were needed as I settled the estate. A Last Will and Testament, birth certificates of both me and my spouse, marriage certificate and the death certificate issued by the funeral home. In some cases only the government-issued death certificate was acceptable. Making a little portfolio of the documents and taking them with me wherever I went was my solution.

The biggest surprise came when I discovered the credit rating **we** had established over the years belonged **only to my husband**. The bank was happy to maintain my line of credit and change the mortgage to my name but only because I had the collateral. Credit cards and other financial institutions were another matter.

We were making payments on our car and, when I went to change the account to my name, I had quite a hassle. I had no credit rating. I finally convinced them all I wanted to do was finish paying for my car.

In regard to the credit cards, I discovered that only the principle card holder has established credit. If I had it to do over again, I would have a credit card in my name as well as some of the utilities. I would also have a bank account in only my name. I discovered that it would have been a good idea to take out a bank loan then pay it back to establish credit in my own name. Women, who have depended on their husband's credit rating, thinking they are establishing their own, find it does not exist.

Certain things in life are inevitable and death is one of them. One may have to work through the death of a child, a parent, a sibling or any loved one including a spouse or significant other during their lifetime. Allowing time to grieve and moving through the five steps of the grieving process is very important. These five steps have been identified as:

1.   Denial - often involves numbness and/or shock. Often a refusal to believe is demonstrated.

2.   Anger - a person will often isolate themselves and wallow in self-pity. They may even have feelings of envy and resentment or a tendency to blame others.

3.   Bargaining - a way of working around taking responsibility for their feelings or recognizing and delaying the changes or adjustments that may need to be made in their lives. Confusion is often a part of this step.

4.   Depression - often experienced for a time along with isolation needed for a time to work through it. It is natural for this stage to be accompanied by crying, sadness, anxiety, guilt, shame and a whole spectrum of feelings. All of these feelings must be recognized, felt, processed and acknowledged in order to accomplish the next step.

5.   Acceptance – only then can moving on to hope be facilitated.

Any loss brings the need to move through the grieving process. For example, when I loaned my school sweater to my sister-in-law and it was returned with a huge snag that could not be repaired, I grieved for my loss. Failure in school or any other kind of loss such as a job, money or security brings grief. Loss may be experienced when we move across town or across the country. Certainly the loss of a cherished relationship is the hardest to deal with.

Closure to relationships becomes necessary for a variety of reasons. Perhaps there is simply a drifting apart because one person has grown through education, personal development or moving forward with their life and the other has chosen to remain stagnant. Common interests or beliefs become so far apart that one person chooses to impose closure in order to protect themselves. Certainly one in an abusive relationship often must chose closure for their protection and including that of their children in some cases, unless a partner can make changes. There are many reasons why closure in a relationship is necessary and only one of them is death.

Knowing that all relationships begin, change, develop and will eventually close at some point helps us to expect that eventuality. The ability to have faith in ourselves and believe that it is possible to create a meaningful future keeps us open to positive possibilities and aids in the movement through each step in the grieving process.

The unexpected in life is around every corner. Expecting the unexpected helps us prepare for all in life that is inevitable. Knowledge is power. When we arm ourselves with the knowledge of who we are, what we are capable of and information that will aid us in preparing physically, emotionally, intellectually, socially and spiritually, we can then live life fully. We can feel supported, fulfilled, safe and loved regardless of the storms of life that come our way.

Recognizing that we are always in a position of choice and that we choose our behaviours and reactions maintains our own power.

CHAPTER EIGHT
OUR LIFE'S WORK

Choosing a career and starting out on the path that will provide us with the knowledge, skills and expertise needed in order to function in that field comes after forming certain expectations. A person usually begins with, "What kind of lifestyle do I want to live by the time I am 30 to 35 plus? What income will I need to support that life style?" A backward calculation is made on how much education will be needed, how long it will take to get that education and then plans made to be able to finance it. Consideration of the length of time needed to establish one's self in their career of choice, and the investment of time and effort to finally achieve the earning power needed to realize that goal, must then be given.

The expectation is that all will go smoothly once the plan is laid out and the path is started. Then road blocks come along and detours must be taken. Often compromises must be made and sometimes even a new career choice made. The marketplace, business climate, job opportunities and all other elements that affect the career aspect of our lives are in a constant state of change. The unexpected is always coming around the corner and the surprise may not come from a bump in the education/career plan we have laid out but it may come from our physical health. Now some sort of ailment has to be factored into the equation. Our emotional health may interfere with our plans as we deal with stress in the way of depression or anxiety.

The intellectual ability which affects our learning and retention of the knowledge needed in order to work in the field we have chosen may become evident as we deal with the stress of trying to succeed. Perhaps we can learn but are unable to recall when we need to. Or maybe it has always been a problem. Perhaps a glitch may occur when trying to apply what we have learned to a new job situation.

Relationships in life often become the reason why we need to reconsider our choices. Priorities will sometimes need to be adjusted if our career is in con-flict with the goals of a spouse. Bringing children into the world puts demands on our time and attention, so priorities change and the focus on time management as well as resources becomes a necessity.

In times past, a career was chosen early in life, training taken and then working in that career was a lifetime pursuit. Now it is very common for people to make several career changes in their lifetime.

A gentleman I know graduated from University with a degree in engineering and worked in that field for several years. He then decided to go for a law degree. Another person I learned of had been a draftsman all his life and when the computer age dictated changes that he wasn't prepared for, he chose to take training in a completely different field.

I started working in an office as a receptionist and was promoted to the drafting room because of my natural abilities that were noticed by the head draftsman. I enjoyed the work but had a problem with leaving my two children with a daycare in order to accommodate my work schedule. After talking it over with my husband, a decision was made to buy a piano and I would go back to the music I had taken in my youth. I took piano and theory lessons, practiced, took on students and eventually became an accomplished teacher of piano and theory. That enabled me to be at home with my children and supplement the family income at the same time.

After about 10 years of teaching music, I began to get restless. My husband was working for a large oil company as their in-plant print manager. He had gained much experience in that field and had worked for many different companies. Together we made a plan to start our own printing business in the basement of our home. The plan involved my going to school to take a graphic arts course. This would enable me to do all the artwork and set-ups and my husband could handle the printing. It started out as a part-time evening business for both of us while I went to school. Then my husband could quit his day job and we were both busy full-time. That was a very successful venture and we ran that business for 12 years.

Then my husband got very sick. At first the doctors thought he had some kind of arthritis. Eventually through searching out many different resources, the real reason for his illness was discovered. He had heavy metal poisoning, caused from the many chemicals that were used at that time in the printing industry.

We had to sell our business at a loss and it took much of our savings to afford the means for healing that were effective for him. My husband was unable to work during this time because of his illness.

In the meantime, our son was diagnosed with severe learning problems. We were trying to help him. At the same time I had gone back to teaching piano so that we could keep our heads above water with the finances. During this time I was introduced to a program that really helped with the academic challenges of our son. I was so grateful for the help and became so taken with the process that I decided to take training in it. I could assist our son and help others at the same time. My motivation really had nothing to do with the income I could generate but rather I could help other young children with their learning challenges and the frustrated parents at the same time. I knew exactly what it felt like to be in that position. So another career was launched.

All my life I had a desire to write and had done some on occasion. After working with children and adults who became attracted to the work I was involved in, I registered for some writing courses. Now here I am writing seriously!

I value all the learning and experience gained in each career I have worked in, but the life's work that has brought me the most satisfaction has been that of developing relationships. I had to work on myself, first taking responsibility for my attitudes, perceptions, behaviors and reactions in my relationship with my parents. Healing that relationship helped me in my interaction with my chosen partner for life and in my relationship with my children. The daily contacts with my friends and everyone whose life is touched by mine are enhanced by the changes I have made.

From what I have experienced and have learned in my personal growth process, it is that our life work is really ourselves. There is within each of us an inner knowing that speaks of our potential and gives us the motivation to develop compassion and caring for others. Loving who we are contributes to our ability to love others. Giving and receiving in a balance is learned in a manner that keeps us from depleting our own resources so we can keep giving to others. In doing so, we become better sons and daughters, better sisters and brothers, aunts and uncles, husbands and wives. It most certainly helps us to be better mothers and fathers as well as friends and associates. We contribute to society in a way that makes a better world.

We are faced with many transitions in life beginning with birth itself. This is also an emotional experience as we must move from a warm protected place into the world where we become subject to all aspects of our earthly existence. The key word here is experience. Since humans are experiential learners, our experiences are key to our learning.

As our bodies grow and develop a change from adolescence to adulthood takes place. Anyone who has gone through puberty and the teenage years, and who has helped a loved one go through this time in their life, can identify with the moods and feelings that accompany this transition. Part of the struggle is hormonal and part is emotional as each adolescent learns that as one gains privileges, more responsibility must be taken on.

I remember a conversation I had with my youngest daughter during one of her outbursts. She yelled out, "I can hardly wait until I can do exactly what I want to, like you do!"

My answer was, "Yes, after I have finished the cleaning, the washing, the ironing, the cooking, putting in my hours at work, helping you with your homework and all the other things I **have** to, if I have any energy left, I can do exactly what I **want**."

The transition that comes with marriage has already been discussed previously in this book. Most couples struggle with creating their own family pattern from their different family backgrounds, patterns, belief systems and in some cases cultures. Family finances are often a challenge as well. But most couples will sort these issues out and then add children into the mix. Each pregnancy comes with more hormonal and physical changes and adjusting to parenthood requires the development of patience and a kind of unconditional love that can only be learned by nurturing children.

Many of our issues surface during these transitions. Working on our relationships and noticing when our reactions to our situations in life fall short of what we would like them to be helps us to identify when there is an issue we really need to deal with. It helps us to recognize when we have unrealistic expectations of ourselves and those around us. Understanding what is behind the unwanted behaviors and reactions toward others in those relationships helps in making positive changes.

Most of us are aware that every time it seems like we are getting one stage of our lives down so that a sort of comfort zone is reached, life pushes us into another stage. As a mom, I pretty much knew I was in charge. I knew because I had brought children into the world, I was responsible to care for and nurture them. I tried to guide and teach them so that gradually they were making pretty good decisions and I could see that they were becoming responsible adults.

Then I became an in-law. It was a big job for me to learn to keep silent. I had been used to voicing my opinion, even when it wasn't solicited. Now I was required to sit silently by and watch my children make what I thought were mistakes. I certainly learned that they weren't mistakes at all, most of the time, but just another way of doing things. In fact I learned a lot about parenting as I watched my grandchildren being parented. I had to let go of the expectation that my children would imitate my parenting style. In the process though, I didn't quite know where I fit. Each of my children married partners with completely different family backgrounds and I have had to learn how to give them space to work out their own family patterns in their own way.

Learning to love and accept the partners our children choose is an important part of our life's work. When you think about it, we are raising our children for 20 to 25 years and they are with their chosen partners much longer than they are with us. I know many people who have or are celebrating their fiftieth wedding anniversary.

Next came grandparent-hood. I enjoy that even more than being a parent myself. One can have all the fun of children without the responsibility. I have often wondered why a person can't have them first. I think I am finally learning how to fill the role of grandparent and it has only taken me about 30 years. Having great-grandchildren is even easier and the labor pains are getting easier all the time!

As each child leaves home another adjustment needs to be made in our emotional bank. Some are easier than others. In my own experience, when my children made what I felt were good choices, it was easier. They may have made a choice to go to university, or they may have left home to another city for a good job situation. They may have gotten married to someone who seemed to fit into our family right from the start, or some other choice that I could see was moving them in a direction that would help them progress and lead to their ultimate happiness. Such positive and logical choices made acceptance easier.

But children don't always see things the way we do. Their career choice or the education path they have chosen may be hard for us to accept. We may have to really work at accepting the mate of their choice, or perhaps that mate comes with issues that make it difficult for them to accept us. Difficult adjustments for us will surface as issues arise, and give us more information about what we need to work on in order to reach our full potential as a person.

The retirement years bring a whole new set of issues. For some it is simply a shift from going to work daily at their chosen career to finally being able to spend all their time at a hobby they have always enjoyed. Others may see retirement as a chance to finally pursue an interest that has had to be placed on the back burner for years and now it can come to the forefront and take bloom.

For those who have had no other interest outside their career, this transition seems to be the hardest. Some have worked so many hours and devoted so much time to their career, that family relationships have been neglected and patterns have been set that are difficult to change. Wives have sometimes expressed to me their frustration at having their husband home all the time. Some will hang around in the kitchen and even begin to give cooking advice. The wife can then get resentful and irritated. After all these years she now needs help with meal preparation? This adjustment is often hard for both partners.

It seems that as people age, the very best in them

becomes evident and in others the very worst comes out. Those that have tried to take responsibility for their learning, choices, reactions and behaviors often become the people others are attracted to. Their support system is made up of many people, family and friends whereas those that blame others become cranky and demanding to the point that they repel everyone around them.

I have come to realize that our choices in life are often influenced by the need to accommodate the issues of others. Sometimes our own expectations of ourselves will need to be adjusted in order to give support to those we care about. The following is the story of a woman I met when around 50 years of age. She has become one of my closest friends and has given me permission to tell her story here in order to illustrate the point I am attempting to make.

Ruth grew up in a loving family. They were a family that society would regard as being in the low income category but as she frequently said, "I always felt we were as rich as the Queen of England. My mom was always helped us to focus on all that we needed to be grateful for."

Music was a big part of their family life and there were great memories of the family gathering around the piano with Ruth's sister playing, Dad on the saxophone and the family singing together songs that to this day, warm her heart when she hears them.

Her maternal grandmother was a big part of her life as she and her siblings always looked forward to her visits. Then there were summers when travel to her grandmother's home was easier and the children were welcome to stay for several weeks. Ruth remembers lazy summer days when she awakened to the smell of hot chocolate and toast for breakfast. She still loves to dunk her toast before eating it. It takes her back to the warmth, love and acceptance felt from this gentle widow all through her growing up years.

Grandma was always sending parcels in the mail. The feeling of Christmas was experienced several times through the year when a package arrived to help celebrate Valentine's Day, Easter, school break, Halloween and sometimes Thanksgiving. Grandma was always finding an excuse to send clothes, candy, paper dolls, writing paper, coloring books, water pistols, sling shots or anything else she picked up to delight her grandchildren.

Ruth vowed that when she grew up she would be a mother like her own and then be a grandmother just like the one she loved so deeply. She knew that in order to be that kind of grandmother, warm memories would have to be created by her through her own thoughtfulness for the grandchildren that would one day be hers.

Ruth fell in love with and married a man who had grown up with a sense of poverty in his family. They were not any poorer than Ruth's family but instead of looking at the blessings in life, his family had focused on the deprivation. After the first child was born it became very clear that it was her husband's opinion that celebrating birthdays and anniversaries was a luxury that they could do without. Ruth had made certain that birthdays for her children were celebrated and that there were celebrations for other special occasions including Christmas, even though she was always disapproved of for spending both the time and money. She always remembered her husband Don on his special days all through the years, even though the only recognition she got was an apology along with an excuse. When her children became old enough they took it upon themselves to make sure she was remembered.

As Ruth's children got married and one by one left home, the problem worsened. Now there were daughter and son-in-laws to remember and then grandchildren were added. In desperation, a decision was made to do some research on deprivation issues in an effort to help her understand where Don was coming from. It seemed that even though the financial situation was better than it had ever been before, Don was getting even tighter with the money. Ruth read, "People with deprivation issues seem to get more and more protective of their resources when there is more to protect."

She tried to reason with Don, but there was no reasoning with him. Every time she bought a birthday or Christmas gift the sum she had spent was multiplied by the number of people in the family and she was reminded of how much her frivolous spending was costing them per year.

It was then that she decided that creativity would have to be the answer. She would just have to think of ways to celebrate all the special occasions, include all of her children, their spouses and her grandchildren with only a minimal drain on the family finances. She would even have to buy her own gifts, wrap them and put them under the tree at Christmas. Her birthday and mother's day gifts could be taken care of by getting something for herself and then telling Don what he had purchased for her.

Ruth came up with her first plan. She would have a New Year's Eve sleepover party for all the grandchildren and then have their parents for New Year's dinner the next day. That way her children and their spouses could enjoy a nice New Year's Eve anyway they wanted to spend it, stay out as late as they wanted and not have to worry about a babysitter or fixing a dinner the next day. The one thing that Don hadn't objected to was family dinners.

So plans were laid and shared with Don to make sure he agreed and invitations were extended. Ruth knew she would have to be well organized if she were to pull it off for the whole event would be up to her. Don always enjoyed family gatherings, especially when Ruth was really inspired to cook a special meal; however the preparation always had to be in his wife's hands.

That New Year's Eve the excited grandchildren started to arrive. There were two girls and two boys. Ruth managed a special kids' meal and then there were planned activities and games. Even the youngest boy, who was only three-months-old, was fascinated as he got caught up in the excitement of the older children. Don enjoyed himself as he participated with his grandchildren. Ruth knew she would have to get the children settled down between 9 and 10 p.m. if she had any hope of getting any rest herself and the energy she needed for the next day.

The older children were cooperative and were soon asleep. However, it was the baby's first time away from his parents and he was harder to manage. Finally, around midnight he fell asleep but woke up after only an hour. There was no consoling him and finally Ruth gave in. She called his parents and they completely understood the situation. They came to her rescue and Ruth finally crawled in beside her husband in the wee hours of the morning. Don was very verbal, "This is the first and the last time we are doing this," he said. And it was.

After that every time a sleep over was mentioned it was vetoed with, "You never learn do you?" However there were many birthdays, and other special occasions such as Easter, Christmas and Thanksgiving where invitations were extended to Ruth and Don by their children and where all were invited to their home.

Ruth then began to feel resentment from her children. She knew that they expected more from her. Occasionally criticism was voiced but Ruth was reluctant to tell them about the limitations that were put on her. She was especially hurt one summer at one of the family picnics she had planned. Everyone seemed to have a good time at those events because there was always plenty of food as well as races, games and special activities planned to entertain her beloved grandchildren. She became discouraged and then discontinued those events when she heard one of her children say, "Mother's picnics are nothing but a dog and pony show." Ruth wasn't sure what was meant by the comment but she knew it wasn't meant as an expression of gratitude or appreciation.

Always in the back of Ruth's mind, however, were the memories of spending time with her grandmother. How was she going to create those special times with her own grandchildren? There were stories she wanted to tell them, activities that they needed to be involved in together, places that she was yearning to take them and share the experience but whenever an idea was proposed to Don it either "cost too much," "took too much time from work," or "he didn't have the energy." Only occasionally she could get Don to cooperate and even come along. Unfortunately those occasions were few and far between.

Finally when Ruth's oldest grandson was in his teens and there were now 10 grandchildren, she came up with a new idea. She would put her stories on tape, and organize activities with all the supplies in a folder. The children could have an hour with grandma once a week and listen to her stories as they involved themselves in the activities she had provided. Perhaps she wouldn't be there in person, but it would be the next best thing. Perhaps her grandchildren would feel her love for them and sense her desire to be part of their lives.

So many hours were spent in preparation for the Christmas gift she would give to her grandchildren that year. She would do up 25 packages with taped stories for each grandchild for Christmas and then the following Easter they would receive the remainder for an entire year of "Spend an Hour With Grandma." Care was given to gear the activities and stories to the appropriate age for each child. It was truly a labor of love.

The problem was that the whole thing was "too little, too late" as the saying goes. The gift was received well by some of the grandchildren, but not by all. When her children were asked about their reaction to the idea, some really thought it was great but others said, "It's just one more thing I have to do, mom." So Ruth decided that she would have to be content with the outcome that had resulted from the decisions that she made in order to keep the peace in her marriage.

The one thing Ruth really insisted on was buying a piano for each of her children when their oldest child turned six years old. Music had been such a joy in her family as she was growing up. It had provided a source of comfort as well as enjoyment for her throughout her life. It was important to her to provide a means for her grandchildren to have music in their homes. It had taken much begging and pleading to get Don to agree but she finally succeeded.

Then, Ruth saw a jacket made from old blue jeans and decided to make one for everyone in the family - every child, daughter and son-in-law along with each and every grandchild. Love went into every stitch and again hours were spent on each jacket. When she was finished 16 jackets had been made. It was Ruth's hope that each person who received one would feel themselves wrapped in love whenever they wore it.

Ruth still tries to interact with each of her loved ones, spending time with them and celebrating the special events in their lives. She never fails to mail off a birthday card with birthday money if that seems to suit the occasion. When ever possible, a gift is still given as it is important to her to remember each family member on their special day. Christmas is always planned for and remembered as well. However, she knows that it is too late to realize the dream she once had. She often thinks of how her mother helped the whole family remember what they needed to be grateful for. Focusing on what she has instead of what she doesn't have helps her to minimize this particular shortfall in her life and brings her happiness.

The lesson to be learned here is that each of us needs to take responsibility to work on ourselves. Sometimes we are required to work around what comes at us from others that we interrelate with. Doing this can help us recognize where we need to make changes in the way we behave or react. Recognizing that we are always in a position of choice and that we choose our behaviors and reactions maintains our own power. Sometimes coming up with a solution requires getting very creative and there are times when others fail to understand what we are dealing with. We then feel judgement. But if we know in our hearts we have done the best in the situations we are faced with, we are not intimidated by the expectations and judgements of others and can continue to set an meet our own expectations of ourselves. In the process, the best that is in us can emerge and our life can be satisfying and enhanced by many positive relationships.

Getting where we need to be so that we have the power to minimize life's shortfalls is indeed *Our Life's Work*.

The good news is that there
are tools to deal with our issues as they come up,
helping us to take care of the shortfalls
from our expectations in life in an admirable way.

CHAPTER NINE
HELPS FOR THE HURDLES

M any scenarios have been discussed and examples given in this book of the situations in life that
one may expect to experience. Being aware of our reactions to situations helps us to identify the changes
that may be necessary in order to get our desired
outcome. Even though we recognize that reacting or
behaving in a certain way often results in quite the
opposite of what we wanted or expected, we keep
repeating patterns that have been unsuccessful. We

even say to ourselves, "Well that didn't work; I will try another approach next time." Only the next time we go into automatic and respond in exactly the same way we had many times before. Of course we get the same result.

Everyone knows that doing the same thing will get the same result. So why can't a person change? Earlier in the book I shared that I have learned that changing the belief behind the reaction or response is necessary before the behavior can be changed. How can one do that?

Many attempts have been made by many people to come up with a solution to this dilemma. The first one I learned of was developed by Louise L. Hay. Through her book, *"Heal Your Body," (ISBN 0-937611-00X, published by Hay House, Inc.).* I became aware that my thought patterns were dictating my experiences. Not only my experiences were affected but they had a direct impact on my physical health. Her book contains a list of symptoms that could possibly have an emotional issue as a base. First I read through the list of physical symptoms in her book and then identified my own. I then took note of what she suggested as the probable cause or negative thought pattern for each. I began to think that she had insights that I thought were completely private and known only to me.

I first tried her method of repeating the positive thought pattern that she proposed over and over. Theoretically, the positive thought pattern would replace the negative one through this process. I experienced some changes not only to my physical well being but my thought patterns. This also translated into a few behavior changes and I started to get excited about the possibilities for me.

At that time in my life, I was a physical and mental basket case. I described my condition in the first chapter, how at 42-years-old, depression had been my constant companion for at least two years, but I am going to re-emphasize it again.

A professional counselor had been helping me and had prescribed medication. I was experiencing severe PMS symptoms and had exhibited signs that I was going through early menopause. Every once in a while I would get dizzy spells in the afternoon and the only thing that seemed to help was to lie down until the room stopped spinning. I also had psoriasis on both elbows so bad I could never wear short sleeves. When I could sleep well, which was seldom, I would get up in the morning feeling energetic and ready to face the day. Then, ten minutes later, a low energy feeling would creep in. I literally had to force myself through the rest of my day.

When I went to my doctor, he tested me for every thing that had dizzy spells as a symptom. I had a blood analysis and a complete physical. He sent me away telling me I was a healthy woman and it was all in my head. Well, he was right about one thing, the dizziness was certainly in my head. Then one night I got up and the dizziness hit me so hard I had to run to the bathroom because I became nauseous. I spent the rest of the night propped up on a pillow on the couch, in a half sitting-up position. This experience really frightened me. There had to be a solution. I certainly didn't want to live the rest of my life this way.

That is when I started looking into holistic helps. Fortunately, I had a daughter who was already interested in this field and had taken many courses that enabled her to give me some direction. So I started with nutrition. I first changed many of my eating habits and started taking nutritional supplements in the form of vitamins, minerals and herbs and at the same time, began changing my thought patterns with the help of the Louise Hay materials.

I began slowly making progress but there were many demands on my time. My husband and I were partners in a very successful printing business and I spent most of my day working with him. We still had two children at home and they were both in school. This particular fall, the elementary school teachers went on strike. This meant we had to home school the children as well as fill the printing orders. This is when our son's learning disabilities were discovered which really turned out to be a blessing for both him and me. In my search for help for him, I became acquainted with and took training in Educational Kinesiology (Edu-K).

Brain Gym ®, as this discipline is also known, was developed by Dr. Paul Dennison and his wife Gail. It was first developed as a process to help children with learning problems but the Dennison's discovered that many other learning blocks are created because of stress.

I must confess, when I took the first class in Brain Gym® I was more than sceptical. I remember sitting in the class hearing about this new system in my body that I had been un-acquainted with. I heard from others in the class that they could feel the energy responses in their body. Some could actually feel their hands drawing together because of the polarity that existed in their hands, just like iron filings are drawn to a magnet. Now I was in a non-feeling place, but still I thought if they could really feel it, if they were telling the truth, so could I. Frustrated with the whole concept upon my return home that day, I decided that I would not continue the course. This new experience was pushing me way out of my comfort zone. It took much encouragement on the part of my husband for me to return to class the next day.

Then the course leader really started getting my attention, but I still wanted valid scientific answers to my questions with regards to what was going on in the body with each piece of new information. I could tell the instructor, a psychotherapist from Denver, Colorado, was getting very frustrated because I was asking so many questions. He was getting behind in his course schedule so he began to ignore my hand when it went up.

When the course was finished, determined to get answers to my questions, I went to the library and borrowed a stack of books on the electromagnetic energy in the body. We were going on vacation and I planned to sit on the beach and read. By the time I got home I had satisfied all my questions. I am a person who, when told I should do something, I always ask, "Why?"

The same course leader was doing another class later that fall and I signed up. The look on his face when I entered the room said everything. "No, not her again." But this time I was very quiet and simply absorbed the information. At lunch break on the first day, the instructor approached me and said, "Is everything all right?"

"Why yes," I replied, "Why do you ask?"

"Well you are so quiet," he answered.

When I was in one of his more advanced classes later that same fall, he confessed to me that if someone had asked him how far I would go with this discipline after the first class, he would have had to tell them the first course was also the end of the road for me. He then gave me a compliment telling me that he now thought I would be very effective in the field.

I have learned that sceptics are good to have around. When all their questions are answered, they are the best supporters of a cause or discipline. They also ensure that there is integrity in whatever they are exposed to.

During the years I worked with the process, having first helped myself, I found great satisfaction in helping others. All who used the Edu-K process were required to recertify every two years to keep up with the new research and the refinements that were constantly being introduced. It is always recommended that anyone wanting to make changes seek out a trained facilitator. You can find someone in your area by visiting the Educational Kinesiology Foundation Website at www. braingym.org.

Many people have become attracted to this process because of stress-related challenges as well as problems with learning. As I participated in the classes to help our son, I began noticing more changes in myself. During the training we were taught a procedure and then asked to partner up with someone to practice it. In order to identify issues that I needed to address, I was asked to single out any situation or circumstance where I felt stress or where I reacted in a way that I wanted to change. We would then form a positive affirmation that would affirm how we wanted to think, feel and/or react instead. This affirmation was to replace the negative patterns of thought, emotion and/or reactions in a situation or circumstance. Each of us would use the techniques we had learned to aid in balancing the electromagnetic energy in our partner's mind/body system so that the new energy pattern supported the desired change. Then, the person who received the balance would help facilitate the change their partner wanted to make.

I was amazed at how quickly I could make changes compared to when I was just trying to change my thought patterns by only repeating positive affirmations to myself. I learned that the body as well as the mind has a memory of all of our experiences. Many times people were able to support their physical health by just simply working with changing their thought patterns. However, there were those who needed to release the negative energy pattern that one takes on with any negative experience as well. Apparently that was what I needed to do in order to speed my healing process. I was moving forward faster when I worked with my body's memory in conjunction with the memory stored in my mind.

Following the first class, a friend, who also took the training, and I worked on each other. The purpose was two fold. We could practice and become proficient with the procedures and we could work on our issues that had been holding us back physically, mentally and in our reactions to our own life's experiences.

My friend and I used the Louise Hay materials until we had worked with every positive affirmation connected to each of our physical systems. Then we started checking out where we stood on the five basic emotional needs. *Remember: they are to feel safe, wanted, needed, loved and accepted.*

Muscle testing can be used to determine when there is a stress reaction. A stress reaction can include physical movement, auditory stimulation such as some kinds of music or other sounds, visual input, foods, elements in the environment, and thinking of an unpleasant situation, among others. The deltoid muscle, which is located between the shoulder and upper arm, is used to detect this stress. A person engages the muscle by raising the arm straight out to shoulder height and then the muscle is tested for integrity, or sureness and steadiness, by another person applying a little pressure on the arm to see if it is easy or hard for the person being tested to hold their arm in that position. When it is difficult to hold the arm, stress is determined as the cause.

Well my partner began testing for my five basic emotional needs. I said, "I am safe." It was very easy to hold my arm when the pressure was applied. Then I said, "I feel safe," and I found it very difficult to hold my arm under pressure.

I remember thinking how silly that was, "Why, that can't be true! I feel safe to drive on the highway, safe to board a plane, safe to experience new places." Then I realized that I did not feel safe to make mistakes or build new relationships and I knew that the muscle checking was responding to the truth.

When my partner and I went through the other four basic emotional needs, prefacing each statement with "I am" and "I feel," it was discovered that I consciously knew I was safe, wanted, needed, loved and accepted, for my life's experiences confirmed it. However, on a feeling level, I was a wipe out.

Sometimes a person is able to make changes with all five basic emotional energy patterns in one balancing session. I, however, had to work with each one separately. That was when I truly understood why I had crashed. I know now that sometimes people can go through life handling one crisis after another and then one day the mind/body system just gives up. The problem was, I began beating myself up because I was unable to handle my life anymore. Looking at what I had already been through, and handled admirably, I was now faced with the reality that one small crisis had pulled the rug out from under me. Ashamed at the fact that I had given into depression, I began telling myself what a wimp I was and that made it even worse.

Now I had a tool for change and was taking care of myself with proper nutrition. Over time my physical symptoms began to disappear. I felt more energy, my PMS actually became manageable and my mood swings diminished along with the occurrence of dizzy spells. At first I could get to sleep easier and as time went on, I could actually sleep through the night and awaken refreshed having my energy last longer and longer throughout the day. I actually began an exercise program and I could motivate myself to be consistent in a daily routine. I discovered that the mind/body system has the ability to re-generate when given the resources it needs. But I found it very difficult to take care of myself believing that I was not worth taking care of. So using all my resources gradually, on the advice of my doctor, I decreased the medication until I no longer required it and my elbows could be again seen in public!

What of this energy system of ours? I learned that there are 14 main meridians or flows of electromagnetic energy in the mind/body system. These are the same as the acupuncture meridians. This system is just as much a part of the body as the skeletal, circulatory, muscle, digestive, nervous and all the other systems in it. Our bodies have the ability to carry 26 volts of electrical energy. The problem is most of us are functioning with much less and sometimes as little as six volts. This is different than our daily life activity energy, but lack of electrical energy can affect the energy we need to accomplish tasks or activities.

Each feeling we have has its own electrical energy pattern. Negative feelings have negative energy patterns causing blocks in our electrical pathways to occur. Positive feelings create energy rushes. Because of the blocks that negative feelings create, we have physical responses to the feelings. For example, the physical manifestation of anger for most people is clenching of the fists and jaws, and occurrence of the fight or flight response. In fight or flight, there is only access to the reptilian brain. It is difficult for us to reason and thus to negotiate or accept negotiation. Adrenalin is released into our muscles allowing us to have more strength for either fight or flight. The mind/body system senses danger and is preparing us to protect ourselves. Some will experience similar physical symptoms during anxiety attacks. Often in this state we are unable to make good choices. Some find it difficult to choose appropriate rational behavior to manage their anger or lack the ability to calm themselves in a crisis. Others may choose to manage the situation by avoiding it, sometimes even to the point of disappearing.

Fear often causes us to hold our breath, sometimes we feel the throat tightening, and almost often there is the butterflies-in-the-stomach feeling. In severe cases, the fight or flight response is part of the physical manifestation.

The feeling of guilt is usually accompanied by shortness of breath and throat tightening as well. Often the digestive system is affected. Physical symptoms accompanying sadness or depression are similar.

These physical reactions all occur because of blocked energy flow. Long-held emotional issues, which constantly block the energy, will eventually cause the physical system to give into disease. Each of the electrical energy flows provide energy to vital organs of the body and are also known as the Acupuncture Meridians. When the energy is blocked frequently that vital organ is more vulnerable to degeneration.

This electro-magnetic energy also affects the central nervous system. Without it, the neuro-transmitters have difficulty firing. This slows down the movement of messages going to and from the brain. Of course this would delay our ability to take in visual, auditory, somatosensory (feeling), or any other input to the brain. This would in turn delay our muscle response as well as our ability to process information and respond to all the information coming to us from our world. When we are unable to process information efficiently, it becomes difficult for us to make good choices. This in turn affects our responses to situations in life and our behavior.

People who are really in tune with their body have noticed the physical manifestations of stress. Unfortunately when I first got involved with Educational Kinesiology I was blocking out the communication from my body. I had decided that if I didn't feel, I couldn't hurt so I had really shut myself off from being aware of my body responses. The muscle checking became very important for me in discovering what was going on in my sub-conscious.

The history of muscle checking goes back more than 100 years. To help me understand the science behind Bio-muscle Feed-back (as it is also referred to), I read, *"Your Body Doesn't Lie"* by John Diamond, M.D. (ISBN 0-446-34278-5). It was published in 1980 by Warner Books in New York. Dr. Diamond refers to Behavioral Kinesiology and Applied Kinesiology and explains how the muscle testing is used in those disciplines along with others. In the book he acknowledges Dr. George Goodheart Jr. DC, known as the "Father of Applied Kinesiology," as his teacher.

Then one year there was an Educational Kinesiology conference being held close to where I lived and I decided to attend. One of the presenters was trained in using an EEG machine and was using it to measure the changes in the brain waves during the procedures and specialized movements that are part of the discipline I had come to respect. That is when I developed even more trust in the science of muscle testing.

I learned that when there is stress in the body the brain waves become incongruent. When stress is not present the brain waves are congruent. The incongruent brain waves take up so much energy that it must be borrowed from the rest of the body and the muscles lack integrity whereas they maintain their integrity with congruency. The muscles respond to verbal or non-verbal activity when the brain is stressed by hearing something that is untrue through incongruent brain wave activity, just as in a polygraph response. The integrity is taken from the muscle because it lacks energy. When stressful activities are performed, the response can be measured through muscle testing as well.

I found it interesting to learn that there are five different brain waves available at all times. For most people, the one that is most prevalent is the one that is most needed at the time to support the activity in the present. We should be in:

- **Delta Wave** - when in deep sleep.
- **Theta Wave** - when in the partial sleep and dream state.
- **Alpha Wave** - when we are relaxing and want to access our creativity.

- **SMR Beta** - when peak performance is needed, we are able to think and move at the same time.
- **Beta Wave** - when we want to concentrate and focus in this state when thinking is needed, movement must stop.

Many times stress causes the inability to move from one brain state to another as appropriate for the present situation. I began to realize why my sleeping was affected by my stress in the past.

Often people want to know how many sessions will be needed to get them where they want to be. In my own experience 10 or 12 sessions saw me through the deep stress-state I was in. However, I wanted to go further because I didn't want to simply live on the edge thinking I would sink back into the black hole I had been in again when I least expected it. I kept working and discovering issues I needed to address, created from all my life's experiences - from my conception to the present. When asked how many balances I have had I always answer, "About 800." Considering all the sessions I have been involved in with my training and then taking care of issues that have come up in my life outside of the work I do, the calculation is pretty accurate.

I want to live my life to the fullest and have learned that when I feel that an issue has surfaced it is best that I work on it as soon as possible. Will I ever run out of issues? Probably not in this life time, although they now come up fewer and further between.

When I was 62 years old, my husband passed away and I knew that what I was feeling was more than just grief. It was then I found out that I was stuck in a stage of my grieving process that was connected to the death of my grandmother. The anger stage. Once I released my anger I could move forward with my grief that was connected with my present death experience.

Several months later I was decorating for the first Christmas I would be experiencing as a widow. Some old issues came up about around being very frugal in my spending with the purchase of gifts for my family. Again, I recognized that there was more I needed to take care of.

A few years went by; I remarried and was living a life with security and happiness. My aunt asked me to help her with some family history. I had intended for years to write my mother's life story so that my children and grandchildren would get to know her. More issues surfaced when I got involved in re-visiting my childhood. They were connected with the feeling that my father was unfair in his expectations of me as a 12-year-old. Again, I was able to resolve the negative feelings and move on to a better place.

How many more will I need to take care of? Probably about 800, because I don't think we will ever be finished in this lifetime. The good news is that there is a tool to deal with it as it comes up, helping us to take care of the short-falls from our expectations in life in an admirable way.

There are many ways to make changes. Everyone must find one that is right for them. This must be something they are comfortable with and have confidence in. Some people choose to use a traditional method like psychotherapy or attend sessions with a psychologist. Many have experienced success in taking care of their issues through these programs. There are group sessions available at many mental health centers where people with all kinds of emotional issues can share their experiences with others under the direction of a traditional mental health specialist. The group support helps them realize that they are not alone and often verbalizing their concerns is enough to help them in getting past their problem.

I have worked with people who choose to work with a traditional therapist and combine the sessions with holistic counseling and energy work. In my exploration of the varied ways available to work with stress related problems, I investigated an interesting, effective method the developer calls, "scripting". Karol K. Truman, in her brilliantly written book entitled, *"Feelings Buried Alive Never Die,"* (ISBN 0911207-02-3 Published by Olympus Distributing), addresses many of the same issues in this book. In Chapter 7, *"Let's Get Started,"* she outlines the method introduced to her by hypnotherapist, Carolyn Lybbert. Karol now works with the method and finds it a very effective tool to create success in releasing and resolving the patterns that hold us back. I highly recommend this book.

A quote from the book states, *"You can do it all by yourself once you have the understanding. You don't have to depend on anyone else to help you. This gives you true FREEDOM."*

People who have been struggling with weight issues for years have found that they must take care of any emotional attachments to the weight before they can be successful in any weight-loss program. Using food for comfort is often connected to the problem, but one must discover the reason why they have this need. Often there are many issues behind the weight problem and each must be dealt with before true results can be achieved. In my experience excess weight has to do with safety, power, protection, failure, humiliation and a variety of aspects of our emotional well-being. Each person is different and has arrived at this point in their lives from different family backgrounds, genetic patterns, experiences and all that has accumulated in their life up to the present. Two people can have the same experience and come out of it with two different perceptions. There are some common denominators in the human race, but because we are so individual, we each need a unique approach to solving our issues.

Just as negative feelings tell us that there is something emotional that we need to take care of (mentioned in chapter three), physical symptoms tell us that there is something physical that needs taking care of. Very often that physical symptom has an emotional base. Our mind/body system only gets our attention when we are in pain or at the very least experiencing discomfort. As soon as comfort or balance is again felt in our physiology, we cease to give the problem our time and energy. Sometimes the problem is both physical and emotional and we need to seek medical attention as well.

I have often used writing as a way of processing my feelings as mentioned in the introduction. I particularly remember a time when I felt my world was falling apart. I was overwhelmed with depressing thoughts and the only way I would get them out of my head was to write them down. Releasing them in this way helped me to have the space to think of more positive things. I kept two journals at that time. One was very private. There was no way I would let anyone read it. I could let my anger out at those whom I felt had wronged me. I could say anything I needed to without having to regret what I said. I could then burn it, use it to identify an issue that was my responsibility alone or help me in addressing the issue with whom I needed to work something through. Often it is best to allow your feelings to process, get yourself centered and then take the opportunity to try and resolve differences with another. You are then in a position to seek for understanding and remain in a state where you can negotiate your way to a solution with that individual. This process is sometimes called, "Writing Out".

I celebrate the ability that some have to work through their issues on their own. Most of the time, using the training I have, I can work on my issues by myself as well. Sometimes, however, I need someone else's perspective with my challenges. It is then that I need to go to someone else and through their experience and insight, as well as my awareness, I get help to discover the negative pattern, belief, fear or anything else that might be at the core of my challenge.

I sincerely hope that the suggestions given here will be "Help for the Hurdles" in your life.

EXPECTATIONS
EPILOGUE

In the introduction of this book, it was suggested that how we handle the difference between what we expected in life and what actually happens, determines the degree of joy and happiness we experience. If that is true, then handling the shortfall in the most positive way is the secret to joy and happiness.

I believe in the goodness of all human beings. I trust that in each of us is the desire to be the best person we can be. I know that there is within us divine attributes that we can resource in order for us to reach our full potential. I have also come to realize that the imprinting we receive before we are even born and that which comes with our early childhood experiences along with all of our life experiences can be positive or negative. Negativity causes us to create coping mechanisms in order to survive in whatever experience we must face. Often those coping mechanisms are tied to fears and negative beliefs that are unhealthy and we must discover why we developed them in the first place in order to recover from our past.

I once had a client who made this statement, "Edu-K (Educational Kinesiology) keeps our past from polluting our future." I believe that the object of any self-growth work is just that, to help us move out of our past that holds us back from experiencing the joy and happiness that is really available to all who have the courage to do the work required to earn it.

In many cases our illness, misery, depression, anxiety, weight or anything else we have trouble conquering is serving us in some way. We must ask ourselves, "Am I really ready to let it go? Does having this problem get me attention and sympathy? Does it provide an excuse for me so I don't have to participate fully in my life or take responsibility for the choices I make? Am I trying to punish myself or someone else by holding on to my baggage? "

If it is serving you, then perhaps you are not ready to let it go. It has been said, "Pain is inevitable. Misery is an option." In reality it is a choice. If you are ready to make a different choice, if you have the courage to look at what you need to change and then do what it takes to change, then you are ready to experience real happiness and joy. When you make those changes you can:

Tap into the power within you to minimize the

effects of the shortfalls in your life and expect to have the joy and happiness you deserve.

ABOUT THE AUTHOR

Colleen Pilling was born in Southern Alberta, Canada. Since leaving high school she continued her education in music, graphic arts, early childhood development and finally in Educational Kinesiology.

One of her most cherished accomplishments is having the privilege of being a wife and mother. She has four children, 11 grandchildren and four great grandchildren. After the death of her husband of 47 years, Colleen married again and inherited three more children along with four grandchildren.

She has written many articles and prepared materials for teaching which include a booklet to supplement the course she taught in early childhood development. The publication was titled, "*More Than a Dry Bottom*" and her plan is to develop it into a full length book as her next project.

Being an entertaining and informative educator, Colleen has been a presenter at many conventions for the school systems in her region as well as a family foundations conference. She has been the keynote speaker for a day home provider organization in sev-

eral centers throughout Alberta, Canada.

Through her consulting practice of 16 years, Colleen has given assistance to hundreds of children and adults. She loves to share her experiences, insights and knowledge and now through writing can reach a much larger audience.

ISBN 142513076-3